VISTAS

An Interactive Course in English

3

Project Director   H. Douglas Brown

Senior Writers

Tony Silva
Sharon Seymour
Pamela Polos

Contributing Writers

Amelia Kreitzer
Bradley Reed
Nancy Schaefer
Jean Svacina
Kathy Varchetto

 PRENTICE HALL REGENTS
Englewood Cliffs, New Jersey 07632

Library of Congress Cataloging-in-Publication Data

Brown, H. Douglas
   Vistas: an interactive course in English / H. Douglas Brown.

   ISBN 0-13-471160-2 (student book: v. 3)
   1. English language—Textbooks for foreign speakers.   I.
Title.
PE1128.B725 1991
428.2′4—dc20

90-44440
CIP

Publisher: Tina B. Carver
Manager of Product Development: Mary Vaughn
Senior Editor: Larry Anger
Development Editor: Louisa B. Hellegers
Development Editor: Tunde A. Dewey
Managing Editor, Production: Sylvia Moore
Production Editor: Shirley Hinkamp
Audio Editor: Stephanie Karras
Design Director: Janet Schmid
Design Coordinator: Christine Wolf
Pre-Press Buyer: Ray Keating
Manufacturing Buyer: Lori Bulwin
Scheduler: Leslie Coward
Interior and Cover Designer: Suzanne Bennett

Illustrators: Glenn Davis, Don Martinetti
Cover Photo: Freeman Patterson/Masterfile
Page Layout: Claudia Durrell Design
Audio Production: Phyllis Dolgin
Photo Research: Barbara Scott

© 1993 by Prentice Hall Regents
Prentice-Hall, Inc.
A Simon & Schuster Company
Englewood Cliffs, New Jersey 07632

Printed in the United States of America

10   9   8   7

ISBN   0-13-471160-2

Prentice-Hall International (UK) Limited, *London*
Prentice-Hall of Australia Pty. Limited, *Sydney*
Prentice-Hall Canada Inc., *Toronto*
Prentice-Hall Hispanoamericana, S.A., *Mexico*
Prentice-Hall of India Private Limited, *New Delhi*
Prentice-Hall of Japan, Inc., *Tokyo*
Simon & Schuster Asia Pte. Ltd., *Singapore*
Editora Prentice-Hall do Brasil, Ltda., *Rio de Janeiro*

Photo Credits

page 22: Professional people—*Laima E. Druskis*
   Asian male professional—*Tim Davis/Photo Researchers*
  39: Eiffel Tower—*Peter Buckley*
   Madrid, Spain—*Bill Wassman/The Stock Market*
  43: Notre Dame—*French Tourist Office*
   Louvre—*Hugh Rogers/Monkmeyer Press*
   Versailles—*M.B. Duba/Photo Researchers*
  71: Condo—*Marc P. Anderson*
  78: Head of cat—*Laima E. Druskis*
   Head of horse—*Wayne Eastep/The Stock Market*
   Inside of typewriter—*Frank Peluso Photography*
   Calm ocean waters—*Olivetti, USA*
   Inside of a piano—*Andrea Brizzi/Steinway & Sons*
   Train engine—*Electro-Motive Division/General Motors*
  91: Vatican City—*M. Bertinetti/Photo Researchers*
  94: The Nile River—*Carl Frank/Photo Researchers*
   Desert Tunisia—*Richard Steedman/The Stock Market*
   The Great Wall of China—*Ronnie Kaufman/The Stock Market*
  99: The Nile River—*Hamilton Wright, New York City*
   Mt. Everest—*British Information Service*
   Mexico City—*Mexican Government Tourism Department*
   Japan's bullet train—*Japan Airlines Photo by Morris Simoncelli*
   Golden Gate Bridge—*TWA Photograph*
   Statue of Liberty—*Bernard P. Wolff/Photo Researchers*
 107: Angkor Wat—*Art Resource*
   Corcovado—*Brazil Tourism Office*
 108: Statue of Liberty under construction—*Culver Pictures*
   Guggenheim Museum—*Robert E. Mates, New York*
   City of Brasilia, Brazil—*Luis Villota/The Stock Market*
   Book cover of Another Country by James Baldwin—*Laima Druskis*
   Book cover of Emma by Jane Austen—*Laima Druskis*
 109: Jefferson Memorial—*Washington Convention & Visitors Association*
   Lincoln Memorial—*Washington Convention & Visitors Association*
   National Gallery of Art—*Washington Convention & Visitors Association*
   Washington Monument—*Photo by Horydczak*
   White House—*White House Photograph*
 111: Tokyo Ginza at night—*Japan Airlines Photo by Morris Simoncelli*
   Hong Kong—*Japan Airlines Photo by Morris Simoncelli*
   New York crowds and shops—*Freda Leinwand/Monkmeyer Press*
   A small car—*Courtesy Toyota*
   A computer—*Courtesy IBM Corp.*
   Leonardo Da Vinci: Mona Lisa—*Scala/Art Resource*
   Icecream cone—*Laima Druskis*
   A television—*Courtesy of Thomson Consumer Electronics*
   A cow—*U.S. Department of Agriculture*

Field Testers and Reviewers

Regents/Prentice Hall would like to thank the following field testers and
reviewers of *Vistas*, whose insights and suggestions helped to shape the
content and format of the series: Julia Berenguer de Soltice, Valencia,
Spain; Walther Bolzmann, Coordinator of Evaluation, *TRANSLEX*,
Lima, Peru; Mary Ann Corley, ESOL Outreach Advisor, Adult Basic
Education, *Baltimore County Public School*, Towson, Maryland; Barbara
Goodwin, *SCS Institute*, New York, New York; Madeline Hudders,
University of Puerto Rico, San Juan, Puerto Rico; Gloria Kismadi,
Director of Courses, *Limbaga Amerika*, Jakarta, Indonesia; Walter
Lockhart, *Lockhart Group*, Pamplona, Spain; Lydia Lopez, *University of
Puerto Rico*,
San Juan, Puerto Rico; Janet Nieves, *Instituto Cultural
Domenico-Americano*, Santo Domingo, Dominican Republic; Jaime Ponce,
Executive Director, *TRANSLEX*, Lima, Peru; Martin Roman, Director,
Instituto Cultural Dominico-Americano, Santo Domingo, Dominican
Republic; Helen Slivka, New York, New York; Daniel Soltice, Valencia,
Spain; Carmen Zapata, *University of Puerto Rico*, San Juan, Puerto Rico.

CONTENTS

Topics and Skills

Rules
Childhood
Predicting and scanning
Organizing information into paragraphs

Grammar

Review: present tag questions
May and **can** for permission
Present perfect with **for** and **since**
    information (wh-) questions
    affirmative and negative statements
Past time with **used to**
    information (wh-) questions
    affirmative and negative statements
    yes/no questions and short answers
Review: past ability with **could**
    affirmative and negative statements
    yes/no questions and short answers

Communication Goals

Asking for confirmation
Giving and denying permission
Exchanging personal information
Talking about past habits and activities
Talking about past abilities

Topics and Skills

Work
Likes and dislikes
Job qualifications predicting and scanning
Getting meaning from context

Grammar

Review: indefinite article **a (an)**
Plural nouns with no article
Verb + gerund
Preposition + gerund
Possibility with **could**
Conclusions with **must**

Communication Goals

Talking about likes and dislikes
Talking about interests
Expressing enthusiasm
Drawing conclusions
Complaining about a job
Talking about possibility and giving reasons
Discussing job qualifications

Topics and Skills

Weddings
Writing an invitation

Grammar

Review: **a, some,** and **any** with count and
non-count nouns
Some, any, and **one** as noun substitutes
The with nouns already mentioned
Verb + infinitive (**to** + verb)
Verb + infinitive or gerund
Present perfect
    with **just**
    with **already** and **yet**
    yes/no questions and short answers

Communication Goals

Congratulations
Expressing excitement

Stating likes and dislikes
Talking about future plans
Making requests and offers
Asking if someone has done something
Saying what has just happened
Getting information about an event

Topics and Skills

Vacations and travel
Figuring out pronoun reference
Getting meaning from context
Scanning
Reading travel ads
Writing an article about oneself

Grammar

Review: advice with **should**
Review: the simple past
Review: clauses with **if**
Advice with **ought to**
Possibility with **may** and **might**
Present perfect with **ever**
Tag questions: present perfect
Compounds with **some, any,** and **no**

Communication Goals

Giving advice
Talking about possibility
Asking if people have been places
Confirming information
Talking about places

Topics and Skills

Public behavior
Common machines
A robbery
Reading public signs
Putting paragraphs in the correct order

Grammar

Review: past tag questions
Review: conjunction **that**
Imperative (with **you**)
so . . . that
Separable two-word verbs
No + noun (gerund)
Past continuous
    information (wh-) questions
    affirmative and negative statements
    yes/no questions and short answers
Past continuous with **when** and **while** + clause

Communication Goals

Asking for and giving instructions
Requesting, verifying, and restating
Making and rejecting suggestions
Giving reasons and opinions
Finding out where people were and what they were doing
Talking about what happened
Asking for confirmation

Topics and Skills

Chores around the house
Leisure-time activities
Getting meaning from context
Writing a letter to bring a friend up to date

Grammar

Review: the present perfect, the simple past, and the present continuous
Be able to
    statements
    yes/no questions and short answers
Reflexive pronouns
Reciprocal pronouns
Too . . . to
Present and past articles as adjectives
Verbs + objects + **to**
Verbs + objects + **for**

Communication Goals

Giving reasons and opinions
Making requests
Saying how you feel
Talking about ability
Talking about what you have done

Expressing reciprocal relationships
Making suggestions
Asking for personal information
Talking about leisure-time activities

Topics and Skills

Food
Likes and dislikes
Compliments and complaints
Writing a recipe
Writing a summary

Grammar

Review: **have got**
Review: **too** and **so**
Review: requests with **would** and **could**
Look, feel, sound, smell, and **taste** + adjective
Look, feel, sound, smell, and **taste** + noun
Review: **enough**
What (a/an)
Negative yes/no questions

Communication Goals

Asking about availability
Asking for confirmation
Making requests
Describing
Complimenting and complaining
Talking about likes and dislikes

Topics and Skills

Geography and trivia
Reading, writing, and saying large numbers
Getting meaning from context
Writing a description of one's country

Grammar

Review: the comparative and the superlative
Review: information (wh-) questions: **how** +
adjective
Get + adjective
Numbers
The with geographical names and places

Communication Goals

Talking about geography
Comparing places
Confirming
Asking for explanations
Expressing positive and negative feelings
Talking about what you've learned
Giving statistics

Topics and Skills

Production of food and goods
Famous people, places, and things
Reading a tourist guide
Writing about an important city in one's country

Grammar

Review: gerunds
Review: **what (a/an)**
Passive voice: present and past
Had better
Before, during, and **after** + noun
Before, after, and **when** + clause

Communication Goals

Finding out the time
Stating rules
Asking for personal information
Talking about famous places and things
Talking about products
Giving strong advice
Giving oneself advice
Correcting someone and oneself
Complimenting
Talking about the past

Topics and Skills

Plans for class break
Transportation
Buying cars and appliances
Scanning and reading ads and tables
Editing and writing a post card

Grammar

Review: **might (may, should (ought to),
must,** and **can**
Review: verb + infinitive or gerund
Review: adjectives and adverbs
Information (wh-) questions: **how** + adverb
The comparative and superlative of adverbs
The conditional with **if . . . would** (hypothetical
situations)
  information (wh-) questions
  statements
  yes/no questions and short answers

Communication Goals

Asking for and giving advice
Giving additional information
Talking about how people do things
Giving opinions and agreeing
Talking about quality and performance
Talking about hypothetical situations
Giving reasons
Convincing someone to do something
Talking about future plans

Keiko Abe is a secretary. She's from Japan. Right now she works in a large bank.
Pierre Blanc is Canadian. He's a waiter in a French restaurant.
Oscar Garcia is a doctor. He's from Spain.
Victor Sanchez is from Spain, too. He's a musician – he plays the guitar. His wife and son are in Spain.

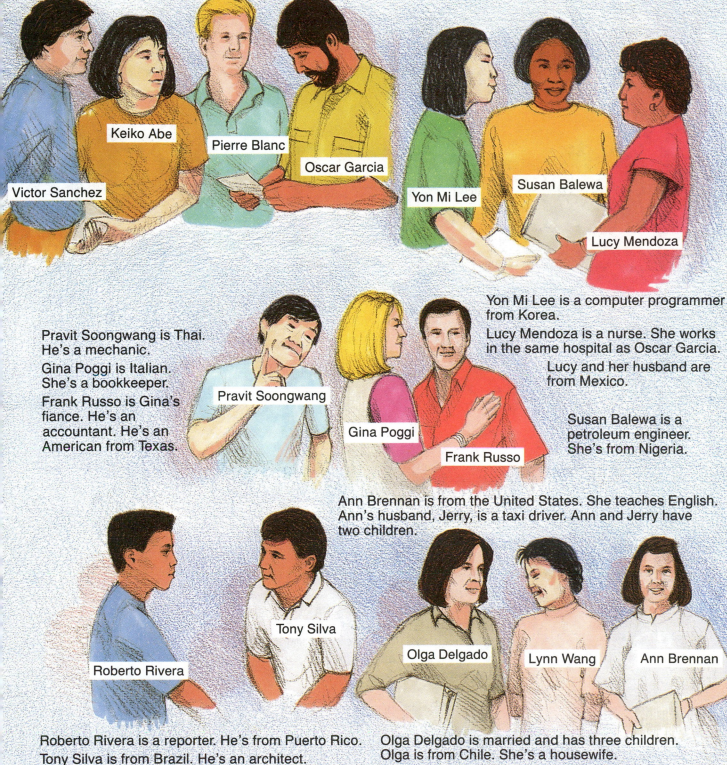

Victor Sanchez

Keiko Abe

Pierre Blanc

Oscar Garcia

Yon Mi Lee

Susan Balewa

Lucy Mendoza

Pravit Soongwang is Thai. He's a mechanic.
Gina Poggi is Italian. She's a bookkeeper.
Frank Russo is Gina's fiance. He's an accountant. He's an American from Texas.

Pravit Soongwang

Gina Poggi

Frank Russo

Yon Mi Lee is a computer programmer from Korea.
Lucy Mendoza is a nurse. She works in the same hospital as Oscar Garcia. Lucy and her husband are from Mexico.

Susan Balewa is a petroleum engineer. She's from Nigeria.

Ann Brennan is from the United States. She teaches English. Ann's husband, Jerry, is a taxi driver. Ann and Jerry have two children.

Roberto Rivera

Tony Silva

Olga Delgado

Lynn Wang

Ann Brennan

Roberto Rivera is a reporter. He's from Puerto Rico.
Tony Silva is from Brazil. He's an architect.

Olga Delgado is married and has three children. Olga is from Chile. She's a housewife.
Lynn Wang is Chinese. She's a photographer.

1

You're from Spain, aren't you?

Listen as you read the conversation. Find out the meaning of the words you don't understand.

Victor: Excuse me. I'm looking for Mrs. Brennan's class.

Marie: It's in room 321.

Victor: Room 321?

Marie: That's right. Are you a new student?

Victor: Yes. My name's Victor Sanchez.

Marie: Oh, right. You're from Spain, aren't you?

Victor: Uh-huh.

Marie: How long have you been in the States?

Victor: I arrived in the States two months ago, but I've only been in Dallas for three days. Are you a student here?

Marie: No. I work in the office. I'm from Jamaica originally. But I've lived here since 1984.

Victor: Oh.

Marie: Well, Mrs. Brennan's class doesn't start until 7:00, but you may go in and sit down. Or you can go to the bookstore and buy your books.

Victor: Thank you.

Look at the conversation on page 2 again. Then answer *That's right* or *That's wrong* and correct the statements that are wrong.

> Mrs. Brennan's class starts at 6:00.
> That's wrong. Her class starts at **7:00**.

1. Victor is a new student.
2. Victor is from Jamaica.
3. Victor arrived in the U.S. three days ago.
4. Marie is in Victor's class.

Complete the identification form for a partner. Use the questions in the list below.

1. What's your last/first name?
2. What's your address?
3. Where were you born?
4. Are you married?

Last name _____Sanchez_____

First name _____Victor_____

Place of birth _____Spain_____

Married   Yes __✓__   No _____

Now give the form to a third classmate. He or she will ask your partner if the information is correct. Listen to the example. 📼

> **A:** **Your first name's** *Victor*, **isn't it?**
> **B:** **Yes, it is.**
> **A:** **You live in** *Dallas* **now, don't you?**
> **B:** **Yes, I do.**

Look at the bookstore rules. Then complete the sentences with *may* or *may not*.

BOOKSTORE RULES

You **may not** smoke in the bookstore.
You **may not** bring food into the bookstore.
You **may not** bring shopping bags, backpacks, etc. into the store.
You **may** ask the cashiers for assistance.
You **may** pay by cash, check, or credit card.
You **may** return books within 10 days.
You **may not** return books without a receipt.

1. Victor _may not_ smoke in the bookstore.
2. He _may not_ take his backpack into the store.
3. He _may_ ask a cashier for help if he can't find a book.
4. He _may_ pay for his books by credit card.
5. If he doesn't need a book, he _may_ return it within 10 days.
6. Cashiers _may not_ eat their lunch in the bookstore.

Make a list of things you *may* or *may not* do in your school.

May is more formal than *can*. When we talk and write to friends, we usually use *can* and *can't*. Tell a partner what the rules are in your school or classroom. Look at the example below.

You can't *smoke.*

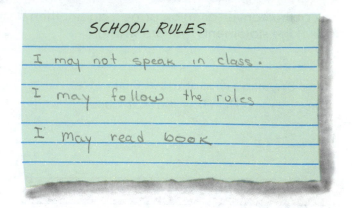

> SCHOOL RULES
>
> I may not speak in class.
>
> I may follow the rules
>
> I may read book

Complete these sentences with *have* ('ve), *haven't*, *has* ('s), and *hasn't*. Then listen and check your answers.

> Victor**'s** lived in the United States for two months.
> He **hasn't** spoken Spanish since he arrived here.
> Victor's wife and daughter **have** written him every day since he left Spain.
> They **haven't** come to the U.S. with him.

1. Victor (not) hasn't worked since June.
2. Victor has lived in the U.S. since July.
3. He has been in Dallas for three days.
4. He (not) hasn't started his English class.
5. He has bought his books.
6. He (not) hasn't met his classmates.

7. Victor's classmates have been in Dallas longer than Victor.
8. They have studied here before.
9. But they (not) haven't arrived at school.
10. And they (not) haven't gone to the bookstore.

Now complete the verb chart below. A complete list of irregular verbs is on page 126.

Verb	Simple Past	*Present Perfect* (have + *past participle*)
arrive	arrived	**has/have arrived**
be	was/were	**has/have been**
buy	bought	_____
come	came	_____
go	went	_____
live	lived	_____
meet	met	_____
speak	spoke	_____
start	started	_____
study	studied	_____
work	worked	_____
write	wrote	_____

Complete the article about Marie Traynor. Use the present perfect and the words in parentheses.

UNIVERSITY NEWS   5

CAMPUS PROFILE

Marie Traynor is from Jamaica. **She's lived** in the United States since 1983. How long **has she been** in Dallas? **She's been** in Dallas since 1984.

Marie works in the office at the Language Institute. (**1.** She/work) at the Language Institute for six years. She speaks Spanish and a little French. (**2.** She/study) Spanish for about nine years, and (**3.** she/study) French since 1984. Marie likes France and Spain, but (**4.** she/not go) to France since 1980 and (**5.** she/not be) to Spain for several years.

What about you? How long (**6.** you/be) here? Where else (**7.** you/live)? What languages (**8.** you/studied)?

After you check your answers, ask a partner the questions in the last paragraph.

Victor is talking to a cashier in the school bookstore. First try to guess the missing words. Then listen and check your guesses. 🔲

Cashier: You aren't from here, are you?

Victor: No, I'm from Madrid.

Cashier: How long have you been in Dallas?

Victor: I've been here [1] _two_ Saturday. I've only been in the States [2] _for_ a couple of months.

Cashier: Really? You haven't been here [3] _for_ very long. How long have you studied English? Your English is very good.

Victor: I've studied English [4] _for_ about ten years—[5] _since_ I was thirteen.

Cashier: Well, I've studied Spanish [6] _since_ I was in eighth grade, and I still can't speak it!

Now practice the conversation. Use your own information.

I used to study a lot.

Listen as you read the conversation. Find out the meaning of the words you don't understand. 🔊

Lucy:	Where are you from, Victor?
Victor:	Madrid.
Lucy:	Why did you come to the States?
Victor:	Well, I always went to American movies, and I used to learn all the hit songs. And I always wanted to study here.
Lucy:	Your English is very good.
Victor:	Thanks. I used to have an American pen pal, and I used to write to him in English all the time.
Lucy:	I couldn't speak English at all when I came here. We had English in school, but I didn't study very hard.
Victor:	Your English is pretty good now.
Lucy:	Not as good as yours.

Are these statements True (T) or False (F)?

1. Victor's pen pal was English.
2. Victor always went to American movies.
3. Victor never learned the hit songs.
4. Lucy spoke English well when she came to the States.
5. Lucy's English isn't as good as Victor's English.

	T	F
1	\	
2	\	
3		\
4		\
5	\	

Say these sentences a different way. Use *used to* and *didn't use to* and the verb that is underlined. Look at the examples.

Lucy lives in the United States now. When she was younger, she <u>lived</u> in Mexico with her parents.
When she was younger, she **used to live** in Mexico with her parents.

Lucy speaks English every day now. She <u>didn't speak</u> English every day in Mexico.
She **didn't use to speak** English every day in Mexico.

1. Lucy's parents live in Mexico City now. When Lucy was little, they <u>lived</u> in the country.
2. But the country isn't the same now. There <u>were</u> farms and fields everywhere, but now they are gone.
3. In fact, Lucy's father <u>owned</u> one of the farms.
4. Today there are factories and highways everywhere. There <u>weren't</u> any factories or highways when Lucy and her parents lived there.
5. In the old days, you <u>heard</u> the birds and the cows and the horses. Today, you hear only the noise of machines and cars and trucks.
6. In the old days, it <u>was</u> peaceful and quiet. Today it's very different.

Look at these pictures. Lucy used to live here many years ago. Work with a group and compare the pictures. Follow the example.

many years ago

today

farms/factories

Many years ago, there used to be farms here. Today, there are factories.

1. little dirt roads/highways
2. fields/parking lots
3. farmers/factory workers

4. only a few people/hundreds of people
5. trees and flowers/dirt and noise
6. cows and horses/no animals

Look at the questionnaire and ask questions about the other people in Lucy's English class. Listen to the examples.

A: Where did *Pravit* use to live when *he* was little?
B: He used to live in the *city.*

A: What did *he* use to do in *his* free time?
B: *He* used to play with his friends and play soccer.

A: Did *he* use to speak English?
B: No, *he* didn't. (Yes, *he* did.)

WHEN YOU WERE LITTLE ...

Name	Place of Birth	Did you live in the country or the city?	What did you do in your free time?	Did you speak English?
1. Pravit	Thailand	City	played with my friends and played soccer	I spoke only Thai.
2. Olga	Chile	Country	went swimming in the river near my house	Yes.
3. Keiko	Japan	City	took piano lessons and went to movies	Yes. A little.
4. Susan	Nigeria	Country	went hiking and took care of my baby sister	Yes.

Interview your classmates. Find out . . .

1. where they used to live when they were little.
2. what they used to do in their free time.
3. if they used to speak English.

Listen and complete the sentences with *could* and *couldn't*.

When I was a kid, I used to waste a lot of time. I never used to study or do my homework. I **1** couldn't play any sports, and I didn't have any hobbies. I was lazy. I only used to play with my dog.

When I began high school, I realized it was important to study and to be successful in life. Today, I'm a nurse and I'm lucky. When I was younger, I **2** couldn't solve a chemistry problem. Today, I can. I **3** couldn't speak English either, but now I can. And I **4** couldn't swim or play tennis. I **5** could cook, but not very well. But today I can do all of those things. And I can do them very well. I can even use a computer!

Make a list of things you can do now but couldn't do when you were younger.

THINGS I CAN DO
speak English
swim

Now ask and answer questions.

A: **Could you** _____ when you were younger/little/a kid?
B: **Yes, I could,** but not very well. OR
   Yes, I could. I used to _____ all the time. OR
   No, I couldn't.

How long have you been here?

EXERCISE 1

Listen and choose the correct answer. 🔲

1. Hans Schmidt has been in the U.S. for . . .	4 mos.	6 mos.	8 mos.
2. He arrived in Dallas on . . .	Sat.	Sun.	Mon.
3. He's studied English since . . .	5th grade	6th grade	7th grade
4. Hans and his wife have been married since . . .	1989	1990	1991
5. Their son was born in . . .	Oct.	Nov.	Dec.
6. Hans has studied music since . . .	1979	1980	1981
7. He's played the saxophone for . . .	9 yrs.	10 yrs.	11 yrs.
8. He used to play soccer in . . .	elementary school	high school	college

Hans Schmidt of Berlin, Germany

After you check your answers, say each complete sentence.

EXERCISE 2

Interview a classmate and write an article with information based on the ideas in the lists below. Give your article a title and organize the information into three paragraphs. Indent the paragraphs. Look at *Campus Profile* on page 5 for an example.

1. *Background Information*

   Where . . . from?
   How long . . . been here?
   What . . . studying?
   How long . . . studied English?

2. *Personal Information*

   Are you married?
   How long . . . ?
   Do you have any children (brothers and sisters)?
   When . . . born?
   Where . . . brothers and sisters live?

3. *Hobbies and Interests*

   Do you play any sports or musical instruments?
   How long have you . . . (How long did you . . .)?
   Do you have any other hobbies or interests?

Before you read the article *English—An International Language* in exercise 4, look only at the title. What do you think the article is about?

1. Many people around the world speak English.
2. People use English for business, travel, and diplomacy.
3. Both 1 and 2.

Look at these questions. Then scan the article and try to find the answers *without* reading the whole article.

1. How many people speak English?
   a. about 700 million   b. about 150 million   c. 40 percent

2. In the last 25 years, the number of English speakers has increased more than
   a. 25 percent   b. 40 percent   c. 10 percent

3. The language of diplomacy used to be
   a. German   b. English   c. French

4. The language of science used to be
   a. German   b. English   c. French

Now read the article and check your answers.

INTERNATIONAL AFFAIRS

English — An International Language

The number of English-speaking people in the world has increased more than 40 percent in the last 25 years. Today, about 700 million people speak English. English is the language of diplomacy, business, science, travel, and even rock music. Many people around the world can get better salaries if they can speak English.

English hasn't always been an international language. French was the international language of diplomacy until World War I, and German used to be the language of scientists. Today, however, Japanese businesspeople use English when they speak to Brazilians. Canadians use English when they work with Mexicans. Italians use English when they negotiate with Australians.

Source: *Newsweek*, November 15, 1982

GRAMMAR SUMMARY

REVIEW: PRESENT TAG QUESTIONS

Your first name's Victor, isn't it?
You aren't married, are you?
You live in Dallas now, don't you?

MAY AND *CAN* FOR PERMISSION

You	may may not can't	smoke	in the bookstore.

PRESENT PERFECT WITH *FOR* AND *SINCE*

Information (Wh-) Questions

How long	have	you we they	studied	English?
	has	she he		

Affirmative and Negative Statements

I You They	've haven't	studied it	since 1985. for three years.
She He	's hasn't		

PAST TIME WITH *USED TO*

Information (Wh-) Questions

Where	did	you	use to	live?

Affirmative and Negative Statements

I	used to	live	in the country.
	didn't use to		in the city.

Yes/No Questions

Did	you	use to	go	to school there?

Short Answers

Yes, I did.
No, I didn't.

REVIEW: PAST ABILITY WITH *COULD*

Affirmative and Negative Statements

I **could swim.**
I **couldn't ski.**

Yes/No Questions

Could	you	speak	English?

Short Answers

Yes, I could.
No, I couldn't.

VOCABULARY

assistance
backpack
campus
cashier
chemistry
diplomacy
English-speaking
everywhere
field
grade
highway
hiking
hit song
hobby
high school
lucky
musical instrument
originally
pen pal
percent
profile
saxophone
science
shopping bag
within
World War I

in the old days
Now they're gone.

VOCABULARY

REGULAR VERBS

increase
negotiate
own
realize
solve
waste time

IRREGULAR VERBS

Present	Past	Past Participle
be	was/were	been
buy	bought	bought
come	came	come
go	went	gone
meet	met	met
speak	spoke	spoken
take (care of)	took	taken
write	wrote	written

COMMUNICATION SUMMARY

ASKING FOR CONFIRMATION

Your first name's Victor, isn't it?
   Yes, it is.
You live in Dallas now, don't you?
   No, I don't. I live in Houston.

GIVING AND DENYING PERMISSION

You may pay by cash, check, or credit card.
You may not smoke in the bookstore.
You can't smoke.

EXCHANGING PERSONAL INFORMATION

How long have you been here?
   I've been here since Saturday.
   I arrived on Saturday.
How long have you studied English?
   I've studied English for about seven years.

TALKING ABOUT PAST HABITS AND ACTIVITIES

Where did you use to live when you were little?
   I used to live in Mexico.
   I've always lived here.
Did you use to live in the country or the city?
   I used to live in the country.

TALKING ABOUT PAST ABILITIES

Could you speak English when you were a kid?
   Yes, I could, but not very well.
   No, I couldn't.

UNIT 2

I can't stand sitting at a desk all day.

Listen as you read the conversation. Find out the meaning of the words you don't understand.

Lynn: What are you doing?

Keiko: I'm looking for a new job. I hate being a secretary.

Lynn: What kind of job are you looking for?

Keiko: I'm not sure.

Lynn: Do you have any ideas?

Keiko: No. But I can't stand sitting at a desk all day. I don't like typing, and I don't like filing either.

Lynn: What *do* you like?

Keiko: Well, I love helping people, and I enjoy having responsibility.

Lynn: Do you like working for big companies?

Keiko: No. I work for a big company now. Big companies are too impersonal.

Look at the conversation on page 14 again. What did you find out about Keiko? Complete the sentences.

1. Keiko hates _____ a secretary.
2. She can't stand _____ at a desk all day.
3. She doesn't like _____ .
4. She doesn't like _____ either.
5. She doesn't like _____ for big companies.
6. But she loves _____ people.
7. And she enjoys _____ responsibility.

Here are the answers. They are the noun forms of verbs. They are called gerunds. What are the base forms of these gerunds?

Gerund	Base Form
1. being	**be**
2. sitting	_____
3. typing	_____
4. filing	_____
5. working	_____
6. helping	_____
7. having	_____

Add your own items to the list below. Then say what you like and don't like about your job or profession.

LIKES AND DISLIKES

traveling
working with my hands
helping people
driving
having responsibility
working for a small company
sitting at a desk all day
typing

answering the telephone
filing
working with numbers
working for a big company
_____
_____
_____
_____

I like
I love
I enjoy
I don't like   *traveling.*
I hate
I can't stand

What about the other students in Keiko's class? What do they do? Complete the sentences with *a* or *an* where necessary. Then listen and check your answers. 🖴

Oscar enjoys being **a** doctor because doctors help people.

1. Yon Mi likes being a computer programmer in _____ big company because _____ big companies have good benefits.
2. Lynn likes being _____ photographer because _____ photographers meet interesting people.
3. Olga loves being _____ housewife because _____ housewives can spend a lot of time with their families.
4. Tony enjoys being _____ architect because _____ architects build beautiful buildings.
5. Lucy likes working as _____ nurse because _____ nurses have a lot of responsibility.
6. Victor is _____ musician in a band. _____ musicians often work at night.

Work with a group. Look at the illustrations and answer the questions as in the example.

What's Roberto interested in?

He's interested in traveling.
He's interested in meeting different people.
He's interested in visiting a lot of different places.

1. What's Keiko tired of?

2. What's Keiko afraid of?

3. What's Roberto worried about?

4. What's Susan thinking about?

5. What's Lynn good at?

6. What's Victor looking forward to?

Listen and complete this conversation.

Lynn: Well, let's think. What do you enjoy ¹_____ ?

Keiko: Well, I enjoy ²_____ .

Lynn: That's a good start. What about ³_____ a flight attendant?

Keiko: I can't do that part time. Besides, I'm afraid of ⁴_____ .

Lynn: Do you like ⁵_____ outside? I know you love flowers.

Keiko: No. I'm not really interested in ⁶_____ that. I can't stand ⁷_____ in the sun.

Lynn: Are you worried about ⁸_____ a lot of money?

Keiko: Not really. I'm just looking forward to ⁹_____ a new job. I'm good at ¹⁰_____ clerical work, but I'm tired of ¹¹_____ the same routine every day.

Complete the sentences about your partner and yourself. Don't forget to use *at, about, of, in,* or *to.*

My partner (name)
is tired ¹_____ .
is afraid ²_____ .
is worried ³_____ .
is interested ⁴_____ .
is thinking ⁵_____ .
is looking forward ⁶_____ .
is good ⁷_____ .

I am tired ¹_____ .
am afraid ²_____ .
am worried ³_____ .
am interested ⁴_____ .
am thinking ⁵_____ .
am looking forward ⁶_____ .
am good ⁷_____ .

This must be my lucky day.

Listen as you read the letter. Find out the meaning of the words you don't understand. 🔲

Dear Mom and Dad,

This must be my lucky day! I have a new job as an administrative assistant to a young fashion designer. Her name is Jessica Holloway. I'm going to take care of the office and help with fashion shows. I've always been interested in clothes so I'm looking forward to working there. I'm going to start working on Monday.

I know I could do a lot of things with my business background. For example, I could work in a bank or I could get a job as a buyer in a department store. However, I want to continue studying English so I need a part-time job. The job with Jessica Holloway Designs is perfect. The hours are good (I work from 9 to 1 four days a week) and the salary isn't bad.

I hated my last job. I was bored with being a secretary. I didn't like sitting at a desk and typing and filing all day. Of course, there is some clerical work in my new job, too. But this is a very special job with a very special woman. I'm excited about working for her. And she must be very successful because she has stores in Los Angeles, New York, and Paris!

Love, Keiko

Refer to the letter on page 17. What kind of work could Keiko probably do with her background? Choose the appropriate word in parentheses.

1. She (could/couldn't) work in a bank.
2. She (could/couldn't) get a job as a buyer in a department store.
3. She (could/couldn't) work as a nurse.
4. She (could/couldn't) be a secretary.
5. She (could/couldn't) get a job as an architect.
6. She (could/couldn't) be an administrative assistant to a fashion designer.

Now say which of these jobs you could or couldn't do.

I could probably _____ , but I couldn't _____ .
OR
I couldn't do any of these things.

Listen to Keiko's interview with Jessica Holloway. What things does Keiko like and dislike? What things didn't she mention? 📼

JESSICA HOLLOWAY DESIGNS
Applicant Interest Profile

Applicant's name: __Keiko Abe__

Address: __431 Lincoln Street, Apt. 4, Dallas, TX 75214__

Position: __Administrative Assistant__   Telephone: __(214) 555-8133__

	likes	doesn't like	didn't mention	interests
1.	√			working with people
2.				sitting at a desk all day
3.				typing, filing, answering the phone
4.				traveling
5.				working for a small company
6.				having a daily routine
7.				meeting new people
8.				working outside
9.				driving
10.				working with numbers
11.				working with her hands
12.				other (cooking, sewing)

Suggest a job to a partner and practice the conversation. Your partner can answer with the items in the Applicant Interest Profile on page 18.

A: Well, let's think. What do you enjoy doing?
B: Well, I enjoy/like _____ .
A: That's a good start. Maybe you could be a _____ .
B: Yes, maybe I could. I enjoy/like _____ .
                    OR
B: No, I couldn't be a _____ .
A: Why not?
B: Because I don't like/hate/can't stand _____ .

POSSIBLE JOBS
farmer
bookkeeper
carpenter
pilot
telephone operator
chef
_____

Victor is also thinking about getting a part-time job. Work with a group and talk about Victor's ideas. Look at the example.

Victor couldn't get a job as a *computer programmer* **because he doesn't know how to** *use a computer.*

What do these people do? Say what you think and complete the conversations. Then listen to the statements and possible responses. 🔲

A: Phil works here.
B: **He must be a doctor.**

A: Maria works here.
B: _____

A: Elena and Martin work here.
B: _____

A: Harvey works here.
B: _____

A: Mike works here.
B: _____

A: Meg works here.
B: _____

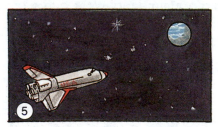

A: Pedro works here.
B: _____

What do you think? Discuss these situations in a group. Look at the example.

Liz usually drives her car to work, but this morning she had to walk.

A: **Her car must not work.**
B: **Her car must be in the garage.**
C: **She must be angry.**

1. It's 8:00 at night. John has worked 12 hours today, and he hasn't had lunch or dinner.
2. Ellen made plans for her vacation. Today her boss said she couldn't go. She didn't take a vacation last year.
3. Steve used to play the piano and sing in a restaurant, but people didn't like his music. His boss fired him, and now he can't find a job.
4. Carol really likes animals, but she never plays with her boyfriend's cat.
5. Paula has had the same job for five years, but she never has any money. Now she reads the employment ads every day.

What are your strengths and weaknesses?

EXERCISE 1

Before you read the article *Applying for a Job—Before Your Interview,* look at the title of the article. What do you think the article is about?

1. The article is about getting ready for a job interview.
2. The article is about different kinds of jobs.
3. Both 1 and 2.

Now read the article and check your answer.

24 **EMPLOYMENT MONTHLY**

APPLYING FOR A JOB—BEFORE YOUR INTERVIEW

Here are some questions to think about. Your answers will help you choose the right job. Your answers will also help you answer the interviewer's questions.

Do You Have the Right Skills?

If you want to be a salesperson, do you enjoy traveling, and are you good at meeting people? Are you aggressive?

If you want to be a secretary, are you interested in working in an office? Can you type and file quickly? Are you patient?

If you want to work in a store or restaurant, do you like helping people? Are you good at working with numbers? Are you friendly?

What skills do you need for the job you would like to have?

Are You Responsible? Do you work hard? Do you always do the best job you can? Do you help your co-workers?

Are you reliable? Do you start working on time? Do you come to work every day? If you begin working on something, do you finish it?

What Are Your Strengths?

For example, do you work well with people? Are you good at math? Can you type fast? Do you learn quickly? Are you reliable? Can you work independently?

What Are Your Weaknesses?

For example, perhaps your English is still not very good, but you're taking a class to improve it. Perhaps you are impatient because your co-workers do not work very fast, but you are learning to be more patient.

Scan the article in exercise 1 and try to match the words in column A and column B *without* reading the whole article.

A	B
1. salesperson	friendly
2. secretary	aggressive
3. restaurant employee	patient

Refer to the article in exercise 1 again and choose the best answer.

1. *Skills* are
   a. things you know how to do—for example, typing or working with numbers.
   b. good jobs—for example, jobs as salesmen, saleswomen, and secretaries.

2. If you are *reliable,*
   a. you go to work on time, you are seldom absent, and you always finish doing your work.
   b. you don't worry about being on time or finishing your work.

3. *Strengths* are
   a. things you are good at.
   b. things you aren't good at and need to improve.

4. *Weaknesses* are
   a. things you are good at.
   b. things you aren't good at and need to improve.

First look at the pictures of the people below and read the information about them in the chart in exercise 5 on page 23. Then listen and find out which person got the job. 📼

Georgia Hall

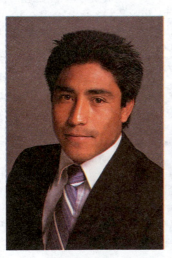

Greg Otero

Susan White

Albert Wu

You and a partner want to hire a new salesperson for your company. The salesperson will sell school supplies to colleges and universities. Look at the chart and study the likes, dislikes, and experience of the applicants. Discuss the applicants with your partner. Decide which applicant you want to hire. Listen to the example.

NAMES	LIKES	DISLIKES	EXPERIENCE
Georgia Hall	responsibility working with people	clerical work working with numbers	worked in a school
Greg Otero	working independently responsibility	large companies traveling by plane	worked in a college bookstore
Susan White	traveling big companies	selling working at night	worked as a bookkeeper
Albert Wu	selling helping people	working alone traveling	was a salesman in a shoe store

A: **What do you think about hiring** *Greg Otero*?
B: **I think** *he* **could do the job.** *He* **enjoys** *working independently*, **and he likes** *having responsibility*. **Also, he used to** *work in a college bookstore*.
A: **Yes, but** *he* **hates** *working for large companies*, **and** *he* **isn't interested in** *traveling by plane*.

You work at an employment agency. A classmate is looking for a job. Interview your classmate.

YOU	YOUR CLASSMATE
1. Begin with *You must be (name)*.	Say *That's right* or give your correct name.
2. Find out what kind of work he or she does now.	Say what you do or what you used to do (or say *I don't have a job right now*).
3. If your classmate has a job, find out why he or she likes it (or if your classmate doesn't have a job, find out what kind of job he or she would like to have).	Say why you like your job and say what you don't like or are tired of (or say what kind of job you'd be interested in and mention any experience you have).
4. Ask other questions.	Answer your classmate's questions.

GRAMMAR SUMMARY

REVIEW: INDEFINITE ARTICLE A (AN)

Lynn likes being **a** photographer.
Tony enjoys being **an** architect.

PLURAL NOUNS WITH NO ARTICLE

Photographers meet interesting people.
Big **companies** are impersonal.

VERB + GERUND

I	enjoy love can't stand	studying	English.

PREPOSITION + GERUND

What do you think	about	traveling?
Are you interested	in	
I was bored	with	traveling.
I'm looking forward	to	

POSSIBILITY WITH COULD

He	could couldn't	get	a job as a telephone operator.

CONCLUSIONS WITH MUST

You		be Ms. Abe.
They	must must not	be doctors.
Her car		work.

VOCABULARY

aggressive
background
buyer
chef
clerical work
co-worker
daily
fashion designer
fashion show
hairdresser
impatient
impersonal
independently
perfect
possible
reliable
responsibility
responsible
routine
strength
weakness

That's a good start.
This must be my lucky day.

VOCABULARY

VERBS*

admire
file
fire
hire
improve
know [knew/known] how to

VERBS + GERUND

begin [began/begun]
can't stand
continue
enjoy
hate
(would) like
love
mention
start

PREPOSITION + GERUND

be afraid of
be bored with
be excited about
be good at
be interested in
be tired of
be worried about
look forward to
think [thought/thought] about

* The past tense and past
  participles of irregular verbs
  are given in brackets. A
  complete list of irregular
  verbs is on page 126.

COMMUNICATION SUMMARY

TALKING ABOUT LIKES AND DISLIKES

I'd like being a salesman.
I enjoy traveling.
I don't like working outside.
I'm afraid of flying.

TALKING ABOUT INTERESTS

He's interested in meeting different people.
He's interested in visiting a lot of different places.

EXPRESSING ENTHUSIASM

I'm looking forward to having a new job.
I'm excited about working there.

DRAWING CONCLUSIONS

You must be Ms. Abe.
Her car must not work.

COMPLAINING ABOUT A JOB

I'm tired of being a secretary.
I can't stand sitting at a desk all day.
I hate typing and filing.

TALKING ABOUT POSSIBILITY AND GIVING REASONS

Maybe you could be a pilot.
   Maybe I could. I enjoy flying.
   No, I couldn't be a pilot.
Why not?
   Because I don't like flying.

DISCUSSING JOB QUALIFICATIONS

What do you think about hiring Greg Otero?
   I think he could do the job. He enjoys working independently.
   Also, he used to work as a bookkeeper.

Congratulations!

Listen as you read the conversation. Find out the meaning of the words you don't understand.

Gina: Hi, Lynn. It's Gina.

Lynn: Hi, Gina. What's up?

Gina: Well, I have some news. Frank and I are going to get married. We decided to announce our engagement last night.

Lynn: Oh, that's wonderful! Congratulations!

Gina: Thanks. I'm so excited!

Lynn: When do you plan to have the wedding?

Gina: We're not sure, but we hope to get married as soon as possible. I don't believe in long engagements.

Lynn: Oh, Gina, I'm really happy for you.

Gina: Thanks. Can you meet me for lunch tomorrow? I want to ask you something.

Lynn: What?

Gina: No. I want to ask you in person. So, are you free for lunch?

Lynn: Sure. I can't wait to hear about your plans. I love to go to weddings.

Look at the conversation on page 26 again. Then respond to these statements. Say *That's right, That's wrong,* or *It doesn't say.* Correct the sentences that are wrong.

1. Frank is in Gina's class.
2. Frank and Gina are going to get married.
3. Frank will be a terrific husband.
4. Frank and Gina don't want to get married immediately.
5. Gina and Lynn are going to meet for lunch tomorrow.
6. Lynn isn't interested in Gina's plans.

Complete Gina's letter to her friend Angela in Boston. Use the verbs in parentheses. Then listen and check your answers. 🔲

Dear Angela,

I can't wait **to tell** you the good news. I've decided (**1.** marry) Frank. We plan (**2.** get married) as soon as possible. In fact, we expect (**3.** have) our wedding within the next two months. The wedding will be small—just family and a few friends—and we would like (**4.** invite) you and Jim. Please promise (**5.** come).

There is a lot to do. We have (**6.** get) a marriage license. We need (**7.** have) a blood test. And we want (**8.** find) a nice place for the wedding reception.

Don't forget (**9.** tell) Jim about the wedding. As soon as we know the date, I'll send you a formal invitation. We really hope (**10.** see) you there.

Love,
Gina

After you check your answers, complete this chart with the verbs in the letter.

Some Verbs Followed by Infinitives (to + verb)	
wait	
1. _____	6. _____
2. _____	7. _____
3. _____	8. _____
4. **would like**	9. _____
5. _____	10. _____

Tell your partner some good news. You can use the ideas in the pictures or your own ideas.

A: I have some good news. *I'm going to get married.*
B: Oh, that's wonderful! Congratulations!
A: Thanks. I'm so excited!
B: When do you plan to _____?
A: I'm not sure, but I hope to _____.
B: Well, I'm really happy for you.

EXERCISE 4

Interview a classmate and take notes. Use these questions.

What do you . . .	Notes
1. enjoy doing in your free time?	
2. know how to do well?	
3. plan to do this weekend?	
4. want to do next week?	
5. need to do before you go home today?	
6. often forget to do?	
7. look forward to doing after you finish studying English?	
8. hope to do in the future?	

Now tell the class about the classmate you interviewed.

Lynn is talking to Gina's fiance, Frank. Listen and choose the words you hear.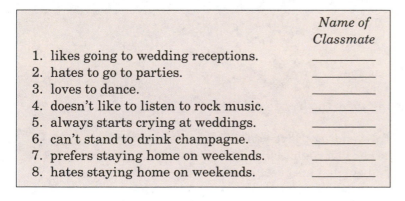

Lynn: You know, I love (**1.** to go/going) to weddings—especially the receptions. I like (**2.** to have/having) a good time, and I love (**3.** to dance/dancing).

Frank: Well, I hope you have a good time at our wedding. I prefer (**4.** to have/having) a big wedding, but Gina wants a small one.

Lynn: Oh, a small wedding will be nice. When are you going to start (**5.** to plan/planning) the reception?

Frank: Soon, I think. In fact, I think Gina is going to ask for your help. You know Gina—she hates (**6.** to organize/organizing) parties.

Lynn: Yeah, and she'll probably continue (**7.** to work/working) until the last minute too, so she'll need some help.

Frank: You're right.

Lynn: Well, I'd be glad to help. In fact, I'm going to begin (**8.** to think/thinking) about it right now.

Frank: That's great, because I can't stand (**9.** to plan/planning) parties either.

Both answers in each sentence above are correct, but which ones did you hear? After you check your choices, read the conversation two ways, once with infinitives and once with gerunds. When you finish, fill in the chart below.

Some Verbs Followed by Infinitives or Gerunds (verb + -ing)		
1. **love**	4. _____	7. _____
2. _____	5. _____	8. _____
3. _____	6. _____	9. _____

Interview your classmates. Find someone who . . .

	Name of Classmate
1. likes going to wedding receptions.	_____
2. hates to go to parties.	_____
3. loves to dance.	_____
4. doesn't like to listen to rock music.	_____
5. always starts crying at weddings.	_____
6. can't stand to drink champagne.	_____
7. prefers staying home on weekends.	_____
8. hates staying home on weekends.	_____

Have you told your family yet?

Listen as you read the conversation. Find out the meaning of the words you don't understand. 🔲

Lynn:	So, what do you want to ask me?
Gina:	Would you be my maid of honor?
Lynn:	Oh, I'd love to. Who's going to be the best man?
Gina:	Frank asked his brother.
Lynn:	It's going to be a wonderful wedding. Have you told your family yet?
Gina:	I called my mother and father last night, but I haven't talked to my sister yet. Frank has already called his parents, too.
Lynn:	I still can't believe it. You must have a lot to do.
Gina:	Yes, I do. In fact, I'd like to ask you a favor.
Lynn:	Sure. What?
Gina:	Would you help me with the wedding reception?
Lynn:	I'd be glad to. Do you plan to have a big reception?
Gina:	No. The wedding and the reception will be small—just family and a few friends.

Read the conversation on page 30 again. Then look at the statements below and answer *Already*, *Just*, or *Not yet*.

	Already	Just	Not yet
1.		✓	
2.			
3.			
4.			
5.			
6.			
7.			

1. Gina has asked Lynn to be her maid of honor.
2. Frank has asked his brother to be the best man.
3. Gina has told her sister about the wedding.
4. Gina has told her parents about the wedding.
5. Frank has called his mother and father.
6. Gina has asked Lynn for help with her wedding reception.
7. Frank and Gina have decided to have a small wedding.

After you check your answers, make complete sentences like the ones in the examples.

> Gina has **just** asked Lynn to be her maid of honor.
> Frank has **already** asked his brother to be the best man.
> Gina **hasn't** told her sister about the wedding **yet**.

Look at the pictures and complete the sentences with *just*. You can find the past participles of the irregular verbs on page 126. Then listen and check your answers.

> Lynn **has just told** Keiko about Gina's wedding.

1. Lynn (ask) Keiko for help with the reception.

2. Lynn (make) a list of things to do.

3. Keiko and Lynn (write) a list of things to eat and drink.

4. Keiko (congratulate) Gina.

What about you?

What have you just done?

Complete Lynn and Keiko's conversation. Use *a (an)* or *the* only where it is necessary. Then listen and check your answers. 📼

Keiko: Is it going to be **a** big wedding?
Lynn: No. **The** wedding is going to be small.
Keiko: Well, it's traditional to have _____ champagne. I'll buy **the** champagne.

Lynn: We should probably have **1**_____ soda, too.
Keiko: I'll get **2**_____ soda when I buy **3**_____ champagne. What about **4**_____ glasses?
Lynn: Would you buy **5**_____ glasses, too?
Keiko: Sure. Do you think we should have **6**_____ decorations?
Lynn: Yes. I'll take care of **7**_____ decorations.
Keiko: Do Gina and Frank want to have **8**_____ band?
Lynn: Yes. I'm going to hire **9**_____ band. Is there anything else?
Keiko: Do we have to order **10**_____ flowers?
Lynn: Yes, but Oscar has promised to pick up **11**_____ flowers.

Work with a group. Pretend you are going to have a party. First make a list of things you need. Then ask your classmates to do things. Listen to the examples. 📼

A: **Would you** *bring the cassettes*?
B: **Sure. (I'd be glad to.)**
A: **Would you** *buy the soda*?
C: **I'm sorry. I can't. I don't have time.**
A: **That's OK. I'll** *buy the soda.*

THINGS FOR THE PARTY
Cassettes
soda

It's the week before Gina's wedding. Gina is talking to Lynn and Keiko. First listen and check (✓) the things they have done. Then listen again and write when they did them. 📼

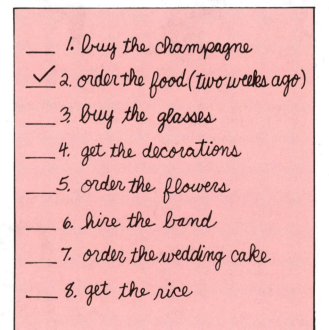

____ 1. buy the champagne
✓ 2. order the food (two weeks ago)
____ 3. buy the glasses
____ 4. get the decorations
____ 5. order the flowers
____ 6. hire the band
____ 7. order the wedding cake
____ 8. get the rice

Look at the list of things in exercise 5. Ask your partner about them. Use this conversation. Listen to the examples. 🔊

> **A:** Have Lynn and Keiko *bought the champagne* yet?
> **B:** No, they haven't.
>
> **A:** Have they *ordered the food* yet?
> **B:** Yes, they have. They *ordered it two weeks ago.*

Now ask your partner some personal questions. Use the ideas in the list or your own ideas. Listen to the examples. 🔊

> **A:** Have you *had dinner* yet?
> **B:** Yes, I have.
>
> **A:** Have you *done tomorrow's homework* yet?
> **B:** No, I haven't.

have dinner
do tomorrow's homework
learn to speak English well
get married
make plans for the weekend

These people are at Gina and Frank's wedding. Complete the sentences with *some, any, a,* or *one.* Then listen and check your answers. 🔊

I wanted **some** mineral water, but I couldn't find **any**.

This cake is delicious. Would you like ¹ _____?

This is ⁴ _____ beautiful wedding. I'd like to have ⁵ _____ like this someday.

I'd love **a** glass of soda. Would you get me **one**?

Yes. Oh, no! I spilled coffee on my dress. I need ² _____ napkins. Do you have ³ _____?

I haven't taken ⁶ _____ pictures of Gina yet. Have you taken ⁷ _____?

No.

You are invited.

EXERCISE 1

First read the sentences below. Then scan the wedding invitation and complete the sentences.

1. Glen and Linda Sue have decided to get married on _____ (date).
2. They've decided to get married at _____ (time).
3. They've decided to get married at _____ (place).

The honor of your presence is requested at the marriage of

Linda Sue Johnson
to
Glen Cummings

On Saturday, the nineteenth of November nineteen hundred and ninety-four at half past four o'clock at the Johnson home 43 Wadsworth Drive Dallas, Texas

Reception follows

EXERCISE 2

Linda Sue's sister had a party for Linda Sue. Look at the invitation. Was the party before or after Linda Sue's wedding? What do you think R.S.V.P. means?

YOU ARE INVITED

TO *A Wedding Shower*

FOR *Linda Sue Johnson*

ON *November 13* AT *7:30* O'CLOCK

AT *Alice Johnson's, 31 Tower Street*
Apt. 9

R.S.V.P. *555-2347*

Now work with a group. Write an invitation for the party you planned in Lesson 2, exercise 4.

EXERCISE 3

What are they thinking? Listen and complete the sentences. 🔲

1. What _____ ?
2. _____ single!
3. _____ .
4. _____ .
   Everything will be OK.
5. Look at him!
   _____ groom.

6. _____ shaking.
7. _____ nervous!
8. Look at her!
   _____ bride.
9. _____ her ring?
10. Relax! You know _____ with her for the rest of your life.

Look at the picture of the wedding and answer the questions.

When is the wedding going to begin?
It's already begun.

Is the bride going to start crying?
I don't know, but she hasn't started crying yet.

1. When are the people going to stand up?
2. The best man is nervous. Is he going to drop the ring?
3. Is the woman in the front row going to start crying?
4. Is someone going to play the piano?
5. When is the groom going to arrive?
6. Are the people going to sit down soon?

GRAMMAR SUMMARY

REVIEW: *A*, *SOME*, AND *ANY* WITH COUNT AND NON-COUNT NOUNS

I want to take **a picture** of Gina.
I want to take **some pictures** of Gina.
I have**n't** taken **any pictures** yet.
I wanted **some** mineral water.
I could**n't** find **any** water in the store.

SOME, *ANY*, AND *ONE* AS NOUN SUBSTITUTES

I'd like a glass of soda. Would you get me **one**?
This cake is delicious. Would you like **some**?
I'm going to take some pictures of Gina. Are you going to take **any**?

THE WITH NOUNS ALREADY MENTIONED

Is it going to be a big wedding?
  No. **The** wedding is going to be small.
It's traditional to have champagne. I'll buy **the** champagne.

VERB + INFINITIVE (*TO* + VERB)

We	plan to hope to	get married	soon .

VERB + INFINITIVE OR GERUND

I	love	to go going	to weddings.

PRESENT PERFECT

*With **just***

I	**'ve**	**just**	**bought**	a new car.

*With **already** and **yet***

I	**'ve**	**already**	**called**	my parents.	
	haven't		**talked**	to my sister	**yet.**

Yes/No Questions

Have	I you we they	**ordered**	the food yet?
Has	he she		

Short Answers

Yes,	you I we they	**have.**	No,	you I we they	**haven't.**
	he she	**has.**		he she	**hasn't.**

VOCABULARY

best man
blood test
bride
champagne
engagement
favor
formal
groom
maid of honor
marriage
marriage license
mineral water
napkin
row
R.S.V.P.
wedding cake
wedding reception

Congratulations!
in person
the honor of your presence is
  requested . . .
the rest of . . .
What's up?
You are
  invited . . .

VOCABULARY

VERBS

announce
congratulate
organize
shake [shook/shaken]
throw [threw/thrown]

VERB + INFINITIVE

can't wait
decide
expect
forget [forgot/forgotten]
have [had/had]
hope
know [knew/known] how
need
plan
promise
stop
want
would like

VERB + INFINITIVE OR GERUND

begin [began/begun]
can't stand
continue
hate
like
love
prefer
start

COMMUNICATION SUMMARY

CONGRATULATIONS

That's wonderful!
Congratulations!

EXPRESSING EXCITEMENT

I'm so excited.
I'm really happy for you.

STATING LIKES AND DISLIKES

I love to go to parties.
I hate dancing.
I prefer staying home.

TALKING ABOUT FUTURE PLANS

When do you plan to have the wedding?
　　I'm not sure, but I hope to get married as soon as possible.
What do you hope to do in the future?
　　I'd like to study medicine.

MAKING REQUESTS

Would you buy the soda?
　　Sure, I'd be glad to.
　　I'm sorry, I can't. I don't have time.

MAKING AN OFFER

I'll bring the cassettes.

ASKING IF SOMEONE HAS DONE SOMETHING

Have you done tomorrow's homework yet?
　　Yes, I have.
　　No, I haven't.

SAYING WHAT HAS JUST HAPPENED

Lynn has just told Keiko about Gina's wedding.
I've just bought a new car.

GETTING INFORMATION ABOUT AN EVENT

When is the wedding going to begin?
　　It's already begun.
　　It's just begun.
Is the bride going to start crying?
　　I don't know. She hasn't started to cry yet.

LESSON
1

We might go to Paris.

Listen as you read the conversation. Find out the meaning of the words you don't understand.

Pierre: Where are you and Simon going to go for your vacation?
Lucy: We haven't decided yet. We might go to Paris, or we might go to Madrid.
Pierre: Oh, [1]that's nice. Paris is an interesting city. [2]It's beautiful. I was [3]there a couple of years ago. Of course, Madrid is very nice, too.
Lynn: Have you ever been to France?
Lucy: No, I haven't. My family was from Spain originally so I've traveled in Spain and Portugal, but I've never gone to France.
Pierre: Has your husband ever been [4]there?
Lucy: No. Simon's never been there either.
Pierre: Well, Paris might be a nice place for a vacation. [5]It's very romantic!
Lucy: Yeah, but [6]it may be expensive. I have to check with our travel agent.
Lynn: What's the weather like this time of year?
Lucy: I don't know. [7]It may not be very nice. I have to check [8]that, too. Madrid might be warmer.

Read the conversation on page 38 again and then choose the best answer.

1. Lucy and Simon are going on a vacation.
2. They're going to Paris.
3. Simon and Lucy have never been to France.
4. Paris will be expensive.
5. The weather in Paris isn't nice this time of year.
6. Madrid is warmer than Paris.

Definitely	Possibly
✓	

Which words in the conversation mean *possibly*?

Find the words in the conversation with numbers next to them. What do these words refer to?

1. *that's* refers to **going to Paris or Madrid.**
2. *It's* refers to _____.
3. *there* refers to _____.
4. *there* refers to _____.
5. *It's* refers to _____.
6. *it* refers to _____.
7. *It* refers to _____.
8. *that* refers to _____.

Look at these sentences from the conversation. The word *nice* has several meanings. Choose the best synonym.

1. Oh, that's *nice*.
   a. interesting b. good c. wonderful
2. Of course, Madrid is very *nice*, too.
   a. interesting b. good c. wonderful
3. Well, Paris might be a *nice* place for a vacation.
   a. interesting b. good c. wonderful
4. It (the weather) may not be very *nice*.
   a. interesting b. good c. wonderful

Paris

Madrid

Susan wants to see a lot of different places in the United States. She can't decide where to go first. What are some of the possible places?

She **might** go to Florida.
She **may** go to Florida.

1. _____

2. _____

3. _____

4. _____

5. _____

6. _____

Look at the places Susan wants to visit in exercise 4. Have any of your classmates been to those places? Ask and answer questions. Listen to the examples. 🔲

> **A: Have you ever been to** *Florida*?
> **B: No, I haven't.** OR
> **Yes, I have. I was there** *a couple of years ago*. OR
> **Yes, I have. I went there** *last year*. OR
> **I used to live there.**

EXERCISE 6

Read the statements about Lucy and Simon. Work in groups and make comments about each statement with *might (not)* or *may (not)*.

> Simon and Lucy aren't going to take many suitcases on their vacation.
>
> **A:** They **might not** like carrying a lot of things.
> **B:** They **may** prefer traveling light.
> **C:** They **may not** need a lot of clothes.

1. Lucy and Simon don't want to spend a lot of money for their plane tickets.
2. Simon isn't interested in going to a beach.
3. Lucy isn't interested in going to the country.
4. They want to go to a big city.
5. They're worried about going to Paris.
6. They can't go on a long vacation. They're going for only a week.

EXERCISE 7

Victor is talking to Lucy. Listen and complete the conversation. 🔲

Victor: My wife has decided [1]_____ next month.
Lucy: Great!
Victor: Yeah, we'd like [2]_____ here in Dallas for a few days, and then [3]_____ to go to Los Angeles.
Lucy: Have you [4]_____ been to Los Angeles [5]_____ ?
Victor: [6]_____.
Lucy: [7]_____ ever [8]_____ there?
Victor: No. She's [9]_____ been there [10]_____ .

After you check your answers, practice the conversation. Use your own information. For example, you can begin:

> **A:** A friend of mine has decided to come and visit next weekend.

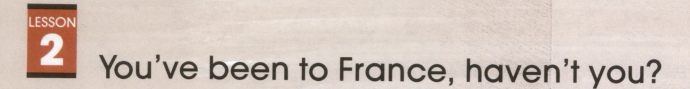

You've been to France, haven't you?

Simon is talking to Ellen Chang, a travel agent. Listen as you read the conversation. Then find out the meaning of the words you don't understand.

Ellen: You and your wife have been to France before, haven't you?

Simon: No, we haven't.

Ellen: Well, then, you really ought to go. You'll love Paris, and the weather is perfect this time of year.

Simon: But we don't speak French.

Ellen: You shouldn't worry about that. A lot of people speak English in France, especially in the hotels and restaurants.

Simon: Should we make our reservations now?

Ellen: Well, you ought to make them as soon as possible.

Simon: Where should we stay? Do you have any suggestions?

Ellen: I'll find an inexpensive hotel for you.

Simon: Do you have any brochures? I don't know anyone in Paris, and I don't know anything about the city.

Ellen: I'll give you some brochures, but you ought to visit Notre Dame, the Eiffel Tower, and the Louvre. Also, if you have time, you ought to drive to Versailles for a day. It's really beautiful.

What is the travel agent's advice? Refer to the conversation on page 42 and choose the appropriate word in parentheses.

Versailles

the Louvre

Notre Dame

1. Simon and Lucy (should/shouldn't) go to France.

2. They (should/shouldn't) worry about speaking French.

3. They (should/shouldn't) make their reservations as soon as possible.

4. They (should/shouldn't) stay in an inexpensive hotel.

5. They (should/shouldn't) plan to visit Notre Dame, the Eiffel Tower, and the Louvre.

6. They (should/shouldn't) try to visit Versailles.

Pretend you are a travel agent (B). Give your customers (A) advice about the different places. Then listen and check your answers. 🎞

A: My wife and I would like to go to France.
B: Well, if you go to France, you **ought to see** the Eiffel Tower.
(Well, if you go to France, you **should see** the Eiffel Tower.)

1. A: My parents would like to go to China.
   B: (the Great Wall)

2. A: We would like to go to Greece.
   B: (the Parthenon)

3. A: My nephew would like to go to Mexico.
   B: (the Mayan ruins)

4. A: My daughter would like to go to Thailand.
   B: (the Temple of the Emerald Buddha)

5. A: My girlfriend and I would like to go to Canada.
   B: (Quebec City)

6. A: I'd like to go to New York.
   B: (the United Nations)

Can you figure out the missing words? Complete the chart.

	one (body)	where (place)	thing
some	someone somebody	_____ _____	something
_____	_____	anywhere _____	_____
no	no one nobody	nowhere no place	_____

Now complete the following sentences with words from the chart.

> Simon and Lucy don't want to go **anywhere (anyplace)** cold for
>   their vacation. They want to go **somewhere (someplace)**
>   warm.

1. Simon doesn't know _____ in Madrid, but Lucy has _____ friends there.
2. Do Simon and Lucy have _____ friends in Paris? No. They know _____ there.
3. Lucy has been to Madrid before, and she's seen _____ interesting things there, but she doesn't know _____ about Paris.
4. Simon knows _____ about sightseeing in Paris. He doesn't know _____ about Versailles either.
5. Lucy doesn't have _____ time to read about Europe. She's too busy with her school work. Simon has _____ time either.

Ask and answer questions about different places. Listen to the examples. 🔲

> **A:** Do you know anyone from *Tokyo* or *Hong Kong*?
> **B:** I know someone from *Tokyo*, but I don't know anyone from *Hong Kong*. OR
> No, I don't know anyone from there.
>
> **A:** Do you know anything about *New York* or *Washington*?
> **B:** I know something about *New York*, but I know nothing about *Washington*. OR
> No, I don't know anything about those places.

Complete the newspaper article about Gina's grandfather. Use the simple past tense or the present perfect tense. Study the chart before you begin.

I was in Italy . . .	I have been in Italy . . .
in 1987.	since 1987.
for a year.	for several years.
a few days ago.	before.
yesterday.	. . . not . . . yet.
last week.	. . . already . . .
. . . just . . .	. . . just . . .

ANTONIO POGGI — 71 AND STILL TRAVELING

I **have lived** in Italy for 71 years. I was born here. I live in Naples now. I (**1.** be) here since 1975.

I (**2.** visit) a lot of places in Italy. I (**3.** be) to Venice, Rome, and Florence. I (**4.** go) to Venice in 1980. I (**5.** go) to Rome in 1984 and I (**6.** visit) the Vatican. I (**7.** go) to Florence for the first time last year. Some day I'd like to go to Milan. I (**8.** never be) there before. I (**9.** not be) to Sicily yet either.

I (**10.** never be) to North America. I might go to the United States next year. I (**11.** always want) to see New York. I'd like to see the Empire State Building, the United Nations, and the Statue of Liberty. I (**12.** already start) making plans to go there. I (**13.** buy) a travel guide to the U.S. a few days ago, and I (**14.** just receive) some brochures from my travel agent.

Of course, I would like to go to Dallas, too. My granddaughter lives there. I (**15.** get) a letter from her yesterday. She just got married and sent me pictures of her wedding.

Simon is talking to a friend. Listen and check (✓) where Simon has been.

1. _____ France
2. _____ Mexico
3. _____ China
4. _____ Thailand
5. _____ Guatemala

6. _____ Brazil
7. _____ Egypt
8. _____ Canada
9. _____ Hawaii
10. _____ Spain

Now work with a partner and confirm your answers like this. Listen to the examples.

A: Simon **hasn't** been to France, **has** he?
B: **No, he hasn't.**

A: He's been to Mexico, **hasn't** he?
B: **Yes, he has.**

We'd like to go someplace warm.

Read the four questions. Then scan the ads for the answers.

1. Which tour is the cheapest—tour A, B, or C?
2. Which one is the most expensive?
3. Which tour is the shortest?
4. Which one is the longest?

Tour A Go somewhere interesting

QUEBEC CITY
4 days/3 nights

$569

• It's the heart of French culture in North America.
• With buildings from the 1700s and 1800s, it is the only walled city north of Mexico.

Day One: Tour of the Old City — starts with breakfast at the magnificent Chateau Frontenac Hotel and ends in the Latin Quarter for dinner
Day Two: Morning — a cruise on the St. Lawrence River; afternoon — a visit to the famous Université Laval
Day Three: Free for sightseeing and shopping

Tour B Go somewhere warm

INDONESIAN HOLIDAY
8 days/7 nights

$1300

• Relax on the fascinating island of Bali — the Balinese call it the "Morning of the World."
• Visit a Hindu culture with 20,000 temples and 60 religious holidays a year.

Day One: Island tour with a visit to Mt. Agung, home of the gods, and Besakih Mother Temple, the most holy temple on Bali
Day Two: Denpasar Museum and market — a look at the arts and crafts of the Balinese artists
Day Three: Free for swimming at Bali's gorgeous beaches

Tour C Go somewhere fun

HOLLYWOOD DREAM
6 days/5 nights

$795

• Enjoy six wonderful days of sightseeing in the city of the movie stars.

Day One: Morning — Tour Universal Studios and see how they make movies; afternoon — visit Rodeo Drive and shop where the rich and famous spend their money
Day Two: Morning — visit Mann's Chinese Theater and look for the handprints and footprints of the stars; afternoon — free
Day Three: Disneyland — all day!

Read the ads above and find out the meaning of the words you don't understand. Then answer the questions.

1. Why might Quebec City be an interesting place to visit?
   It may be interesting because (it's/there are/you can) _____ .

2. Why might Bali be an interesting place to visit?
3. Why might Hollywood be an interesting place to visit?
4. Ask about a partner's country or city.

Listen and complete the conversation. 📼

Customer A: ^{1}_____ .
Travel Agent: Have you ever been to Bali?
Customer B: ^{2}_____ .
Travel Agent: Well, Bali may be a good place to go. It's a fascinating island with 20,000 temples and gorgeous beaches.
Customer B: ^{3}_____ .
Customer A: And we don't know anyone there.
Travel Agent: ^{4}_____ . There are a lot of tourists there. And the people are very friendly.
Customer A: Well, it sounds nice.
Travel Agent: It is. And if you decide to go, ^{5}_____ the Denpasar Museum and market.

Now work in a group. One of you is a travel agent. Your classmates are customers. Use one of the travel ads and practice the conversation above.

Make a list of the continents your classmates have and haven't visited. Use the conversation below as an example. 📼

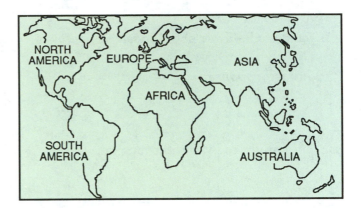

A: **You've been to** *South America*, **haven't you?**
B: **Yes, I have. I've been to** *Brazil and Peru.* OR
Yes, I used to live in *Colombia.* OR
No, I haven't.

A: **You haven't been to** *Australia*, **have you?**
B: **No, I haven't.** OR
Yes, I have. I was there *a few years ago.*

Answer the questions below and write a newspaper article about yourself. Use the article on page 45 as an example.

Paragraph 1—The country and city you live in
How long have you lived in (country)?
What city do you live in?
How long have you lived in (city)?

Paragraph 2—Places you have and haven't visited in the country you live in
What cities or special places have you visited?
When did you go to each place?
What did you see and like in each place?
Name a place you haven't been to yet that you'd like to visit.

Paragraph 3—A continent and country you haven't visited
Name a continent you've never been to.
Name one of the countries or cities there that you've always wanted to visit.
Say what you'd like to see or do in that country or city.

REVIEW: ADVICE WITH *SHOULD*

Simon and Lucy **should go** to France.
You **shouldn't worry** about speaking French.

REVIEW: THE SIMPLE PAST

I **went** to Venice in 1980.
I **got** a letter yesterday.

REVIEW: CLAUSES WITH *IF*

If you **go** to Bali, you **should visit** the museum.

ADVICE WITH *OUGHT TO*

I We You They He She	**ought to**	**visit**	the museum.

POSSIBILITY WITH *MAY* AND *MIGHT*

I We You They He She	**might** (**not**) **may**	**go**	to the Grand Canyon.

PRESENT PERFECT WITH *EVER*

Have	you	**ever**	**been**	to Florida (before)?	Yes, I have.
Has	she				No, she hasn't.

TAG QUESTIONS: PRESENT PERFECT

You've been to France,	**haven't you?**	Yes, I have. (No, I haven't.)
She's been to France,	**hasn't she?**	Yes, she has. (No, she hasn't.)
You haven't been to Australia,	**have you?**	No, I haven't. (Yes, I have.)
Simon hasn't been to Australia,	**has he?**	No, he hasn't. (Yes, he has.)

COMPOUNDS WITH *SOME, ANY,* AND *NO*

someone (somebody)	somewhere (someplace)	something
anyone (anybody)	anywhere (anyplace)	anything
no one (nobody)	nowhere (no place)	nothing

Do Simon and Lucy know **anyone** in Paris or Madrid?
They know **someone** in Madrid, but they don't know **anyone** in Paris.
They know **something** about Madrid, but they know **nothing** about Paris.

culture
especially
fascinating
footprint
god
gorgeous
handprint
Hindu
holy
inexpensive
light
magnificent
market
perfect
plan
religious
suggestion
temple
walled city

a friend of mine
arts and crafts
It sounds nice.
the rich and
  famous

CONTINENTS
Africa
Asia
Australia
Europe
North America
South America

TRAVEL
cruise
brochure
plane ticket
reservation
sightseeing
tour
tourist
travel guide

GIVING ADVICE
My wife and I would like to go to France.
> Well, if you go to France, you ought to see the Eiffel Tower.
> You should visit the Louvre.
> You shouldn't worry about speaking French.

TALKING ABOUT POSSIBILITY
Where are you thinking about going on your next vacation?
> I might go to the Grand Canyon.

Bali might be a good place to visit.
It might be interesting because there are 20,000 temples.

ASKING IF PEOPLE HAVE BEEN PLACES
Have you ever been to Los Angeles before?
> Yes, I have. I went there last year.
> I used to live there.
> No, I haven't.

CONFIRMING INFORMATION
You've been to South America, haven't you?
> Yes, I have. I've been to Brazil and Peru.
But you haven't been to Australia, have you?
> No, I haven't.

TALKING ABOUT PLACES
Do you know anyone from Tokyo or Hong Kong?
> I know someone from Tokyo, but I don't know anyone
> from Hong Kong.
> No, I don't know anyone from there.
Do you know anything about New York or Washington?
> I know something about New York, but I know nothing about
> Washington.
> No, I don't know anything about those places.

No winding and no focusing

Listen as you read the conversation. Find out the meaning of the words you don't understand.

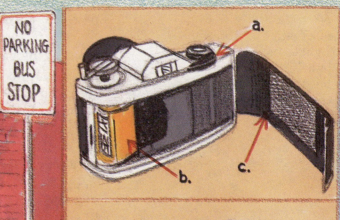

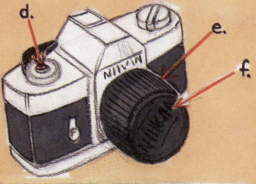

Roberto: Hey, Tony! There's no parking there. It's a bus stop.

Tony: Huh? Oh, you're right. I didn't see the sign. What's that?

Roberto: A new camera.

Tony: Let's see.

Roberto: It's great. It's a Photomax. It's all automatic. There's no winding and no focusing.

Tony: How does it work?

Roberto: It's easy. You put the film in here, close the camera, and it winds automatically. Then you take the lens cover off, aim, and just push this button.

Tony: Well, I've just picked up two tickets for the football game on Saturday. Why don't you come with me and try out your camera? I believe it's going to be a good game.

Roberto: I think that's a great idea. Thanks.

Match the sentences on the left with the sentences on the right.

1. There's no parking there.
2. There's no winding or focusing.
3. It's all automatic.
4. I've just picked up two tickets for the football game.

a. You don't have to wind or focus it.
b. You can't park there.
c. I just bought two tickets for the football game.
d. It winds and focuses automatically.

Match these sentences with the letters in the illustration on page 50.

1. __b__ You put the film in here.
2. _____ Close the camera.
3. _____ It winds automatically.
4. _____ You take the lens cover off.
5. _____ It focuses automatically.
6. _____ Just push this button.

Now point to the illustration of the camera and tell your partner how to use it. You can use these words: *first*, *next*, *and*, and *then*.

Match the signs with the sentences.

__b__ 1. You can't smoke here.
_____ 2. You may not swim here.
_____ 3. You can't bring a dog in here.
_____ 4. You can't go out here.

_____ 5. You may not throw garbage here.
_____ 6. You can't play ball here.
_____ 7. You may not play a radio here.
_____ 8. You may not talk here.

Practice this conversation. Use the cues. 🔈

A: Let's *have a cigarette.*
B: There's *no smoking in the classroom.*
A: Oh.

1. A: go swimming
   B: swim in the lake

2. A: park here
   B: park at the bus stop

3. A: play baseball
   B: play ball in the park

4. A: talk about school
   B: talk in the theater

Ann Brennan's students are taking a break. They are going to watch a short film about the capital of the United States—Washington, D.C. Complete the sentences with the words in parentheses. There are two ways to complete each sentence. Read each answer two ways, once with the object after the two-word verb and once with the object between the verb and the preposition. First listen to the examples.

> **Mrs. Brennan:** All right, Keiko, **pull down the window shades (pull the window shades down).**

Keiko:	Great! I can't wait to see this film. I love Washington.
Mrs. Brennan:	Lucy, (**1.** try out/the VCR). And Lynn, please (**2.** turn off/your radio).
Lucy:	Mrs. Brennan, the VCR doesn't work. There's no picture!
Mrs. Brennan:	Lucy, you have to (**3.** put in/the cassette).
Lucy:	Oh, of course.
Mrs. Brennan:	Just a minute. Pravit, (**4.** take off/your hat) so the other students can see. And Pierre, please (**5.** put on/your shoe).
Pierre:	Sorry, Mrs. Brennan. My foot hurts.
Mrs. Brennan:	One more thing. When we finish, I want you all to (**6.** pick up/these soda cans and all this garbage).
Students:	Yes, Mrs. Brennan.
Mrs. Brennan:	Victor, please (**7.** take out/your pen) and (**8.** write down/a few notes) about the film.
Victor:	Sure.
Mrs. Brennan:	Good. Now, (**9.** turn on/the VCR).

Now listen to the conversations.

One of the other teachers at the Language Institute isn't very polite. Listen and write down the teacher's orders. 📼

1. All right. _____
2. Now _____
3. Good. Now _____
4. Wait a minute. Hey, you! _____
5. And _____

6. And you! _____
7. OK. No, wait! First _____
8. Good. Now _____
9. John! _____
10. OK. Ready? _____

After you check your answers, change the orders to polite requests and practice this conversation. First listen to the example.

A: **Would you** *pull the window shades down,* **please?**
B: *The window shades?*
A: **Yes.** *Pull them down,* **please.**

Point to the illustrations and tell a partner how to use these things. Listen to the examples. 📼

A: **How does this** *copy machine* **work?**
B: **(You)** *turn the machine on here.* **Then (you)** *place the original here.* **(You)** . . . .

copy machine

3. Select the number of copies you want.
4. Push the START button.
1. Turn the machine on/off here.
2. Place the original here.
5. Pick your copies up here.

computer

4. Wait until a program comes up on the screen.
1. Turn the machine on/off here.
5. Follow the directions you see on the screen.
2. Put a diskette in the disk drive.
3. Hit the ENTER key.

cassette player

2. Put a cassette in.
4. Turn the volume up or down.
1. Push the EJECT button here.
3. Push the PLAY or RECORD button.
5. Listen or record.

video cassette recorder (VCR)

5. Watch the video or record the TV program.
1. Turn the TV on/off here.
2. Turn the VCR on/off here.
4. Push the PLAY or RECORD button.
3. Put the cassette in.

How was the game?

On Sunday afternoon Tony and Roberto went to visit Pravit. Listen as you read the conversation. Find out the meaning of the words you don't understand.

Tony: We called you after the game yesterday, but no one answered.

Pravit: I was probably washing my car or cleaning the garage when you called. I guess I was so busy that I didn't hear the phone.

Roberto: Where was your wife?

Pravit: While I was working around the house, San was working at the museum. She works there Saturday and Sunday afternoons. She's a security guard.

Roberto: I didn't know that.

Pravit: Yeah, she's worked there for about a month. So, how was the game?

Tony: Great. Really great. The Cowboys won. I can't wait to go next week. And Roberto got some great pictures.

Roberto: Oh, no!

Tony: What's the matter?

Roberto: I just remembered. I forgot to take the lens cover off while I was taking pictures.

Tony: You're kidding!

Roberto: No. And there was no film in the camera either.

Look at the conversation on page 54 again. Answer True (T) or False (F) and correct the false statements.

	T	F
1. Roberto, Tony, and Pravit went to a football game on Saturday.		
2. Pravit and his wife worked yesterday afternoon.		
3. Pravit didn't hear his phone because he was busy.		
4. Roberto knew that San worked as a security guard at the museum.		
5. Roberto forgot to take pictures of the football game.		

What's your opinion? Give reasons for your opinion.

A: Does Tony love football?
B: **I think Tony loves football because he thought the game was great and because he can't wait to go next week.**

1. Has Roberto had a lot of experience with cameras?
   I (don't) think (that) _____
2. Do Pravit and his wife work hard on weekends?
   I (don't) believe (that) _____

Answer the questions a different way by combining the sentences. Then listen and check your answers.

A: Why didn't you answer the phone?
B: I was very busy. I didn't hear it.
   I was so busy (that) I didn't hear it.

1. A: Why doesn't he play basketball often?
   B: He's very busy with his new job. He doesn't have time.
2. A: Why are they so upset?
   B: They played tennis very badly. They didn't win one game.
3. A: Do you think he'll do well in English?
   B: He tries very hard. I think he'll do very well.
4. A: What's the matter with Alice?
   B: She ate very little. She got sick.
5. A: You're angry, aren't you?
   B: I'm very angry. I don't want to talk about it.
6. A: What did she do after the tennis game?
   B: She was very tired. She couldn't wait to go to bed.

Tony and Roberto were watching a football game at 4:00 yesterday afternoon. What about their friends? Listen and match the two parts of the sentences.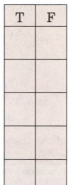

1. Pravit was
2. Pravit's wife was
3. Olga was
4. Oscar was
5. Lynn and Keiko were
6. Gina and Frank were
7. Lucy was
8. Victor was

a. washing his car at 4:00 yesterday afternoon.
b. playing tennis.
c. working in the garden.
d. studying.
e. working at the museum at that time.
f. cooking dinner.
g. reading a magazine.
h. watching TV.

After you check your answers, ask questions about the people above. Listen to the examples.

A: **Was** *Pravit washing his car at 4:00 yesterday afternoon?*
B: **Yes, he was.**

A: **Was** *his wife working at home?*
B: **No, she wasn't.**

Look at the examples and make new sentences by combining sentences from exercise 4. Notice the comma in the second example.

> Tony and Roberto **were watching** a football game **while** Pravit **was washing** his car.
> OR
> **While** Tony and Roberto **were watching** a football game, Pravit **was washing** his car.

1. Combine sentences 1 and 2 in exercise 4.
2. Combine sentences 3 and 4.
3. Combine sentences 5 and 6.
4. Combine sentences 7 and 8.

Work with a group and practice the conversation. Take notes about each person. Listen to the examples. 🔊

> A: **Where were you** at 7:00 last night?
> B: **I was** at home.
> A: **What were you doing?**
> B: **I was** studying. (**I wasn't doing anything.**)

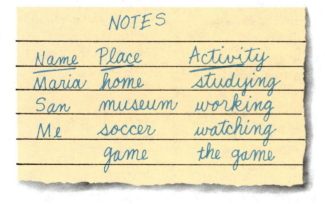

NOTES

Name	Place	Activity
Maria	home	studying
San	museum	working
Me	soccer game	watching the game

Make sentences from your notes and report your findings to the class.

> At 7:00 last night, I was watching a soccer game. **While I was watching** the game, Maria **was studying** and San **was working**.

Pravit wrote a letter to his parents. Find the word *when* in each sentence. Then complete the sentences with the past continuous tense *(was/were doing)* or the simple past tense *(did)*.

Dear Mom and Dad,
  Sunday wasn't a lucky day for us. Tony and Roberto **were visiting** me on Sunday afternoon when it **began** to rain. We (1. run) to the house when I (2. trip) on Kanya's bicycle and (3. fall). When I (4. get up), my leg (5. bleed). Tony and Roberto (6. help) me into the house when the phone (7. ring). When I (8. pick up) the phone, San (9. cry). She (10. work) in the museum when the lights (11. go out) and someone (12. steal) a painting.
  What a day!

  Love,
  Pravit

After you check your answers, ask questions about the letter. Listen to the example. 🔊

> A: **What were** Tony and Roberto **doing when it began** to rain?
> B: They **were visiting** Pravit.

Who stole the painting?

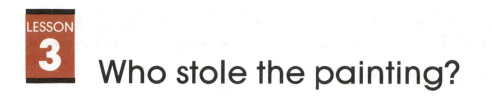

EXERCISE 1

It's 3:59 on Sunday afternoon. What are the people doing?

EXERCISE 2

At 4:00 someone turned the lights off in the museum. What were the people doing when the lights went out? Listen and answer True (T) or False (F). 🔲

	T	F
1. The woman with the big bag . . .		
2. The man with the mustache . . .		
3. The young man with the brochure . . .		
4. The woman and the little boy . . .		
5. The girl with the doll . . .		
6. The man in the wheelchair . . .		
7. The woman with the notebook . . .		
8. The elderly man and woman . . .		

Ask and answer questions about the picture in exercise 1. Listen to the examples. 📼

> **A:** **What was** *the security guard* **doing when** *the lights went out*?
> **B:** *She was sitting in a chair.*
>
> **A:** **What were** *the elderly man and woman* **doing while** *the security guard was sitting in a chair*?
> **B:** *They were standing near the restrooms.*

Don't forget to ask about YOU.

The security guard has turned the lights on in the museum, and a police officer has arrived. Look at this picture and the picture on page 57. Describe the scene and tell the officer what is different.

> When the lights went out, the security guard was sitting in a chair. Now she is standing by the light switch.
>
> There was a NO SMOKING sign on the wall when the lights went out. Now it isn't there.

The police officer wrote down four important facts. Do you know what they were? Work with a group and write down two more facts that you think are important.

Who does your group think stole the painting? Who stole the purse? Who turned the lights off? Present your group's ideas to the class like this:

> We believe/think (that) _____
> because/so _____.

POLICE REPORT

1. Someone stole a painting and a purse.
2. The man in the wheelchair can walk. When the lights went out he was sitting in his chair. Now he is standing near the elevator.
3. _____.
4. _____.

The paragraphs in the newspaper article are not in the right order. Renumber the paragraphs. For example, paragraph 3 should be the first paragraph.

Complete these questions and answer them. Refer to the newspaper article. Then listen and check your answers. 📼

> A: There was a murder yesterday, **wasn't there**?
> B: **No, there wasn't.** There was a robbery.

1. A: The painting is worth $200,000, _____?
   B: _____

2. A: Horton was sitting in a wheelchair, _____?
   B: _____

3. A: Riggs wasn't sitting in a wheelchair, _____?
   B: _____

4. A: The police arrested Horton, _____?
   B: _____

5. A: The police didn't arrest Riggs, _____?
   B: _____

6. Ask your own question.

PAINTING AND PURSE STOLEN FROM MUSEUM

(1) A second robbery took place in the museum that afternoon. While Horton and Riggs were stealing the painting, Charles Seng stole a purse. Seng didn't get far. He fell and broke his leg while he was climbing out the window. Seng told the police that he found the purse while he was walking near the museum. But the police found Seng's fingerprints on the window and on a brochure in the museum. The police still do not know who turned off the lights.

(2) Riggs got on the elevator with the painting. However, the elevator door opened and closed so fast that Horton couldn't get on. The police arrested Horton while he was still in the museum. They have not found Riggs yet.

(3) Dallas - Yesterday afternoon, Henrietta Riggs of Houston and an accomplice, famous robber J.J. Horton, also of Houston, stole a valuable painting (it is worth $250,000) from the Dallas Museum.

(4) Riggs was carrying a large bag and was waiting for the elevator when the lights went out. Horton was sitting in a wheelchair and pretending that he couldn't walk. While Riggs was waiting for the elevator, Horton got up, took the painting off the wall, and put it in her bag.

REVIEW: PAST TAG QUESTIONS

The painting cost $200,000, **didn't it?**
   No, it didn't. It cost $250,000.
Horton was sitting in a wheelchair, **wasn't he?**
   Yes, he was.

REVIEW: CONJUNCTION *THAT*

I don't think (**that**) Roberto has a lot of experience with cameras because he forgot to put the film in.

I believe (**that**) Pravit and his wife work hard.

IMPERATIVE *(WITH YOU)*

(**You**) **turn** the machine **on** here.

SO . . . *(THAT)*

I was **so** busy (**that**) I didn't hear the phone.

SEPARABLE TWO-WORD VERBS

	pull	the window shades	**down?**
Would you please	**pull down**	the window shades?	
	pull	them	**down?**

NO + NOUN (GERUND)

There's **no smoking** in the theater.

PAST CONTINUOUS

Information (Wh-) Questions

What	**were**	you we they	**doing**	at 7:00?
	was	he she		

Affirmative and Negative Statements

I	**was (wasn't)**	
We They	**were (weren't)**	**studying.**
He She	**was (wasn't)**	

Yes/No Questions

Was	it	**raining**	at 4:00?
Were	Gina and Frank	**watching**	TV?

Short Answers

Yes,	it **was.**		No,	it **wasn't.**
	they **were.**			they **weren't.**

PAST CONTINUOUS WITH *WHEN* AND *WHILE* + CLAUSE

What **were** you **doing** I **was waiting** for the elevator	**when**	the lights **went out?** the lights **went out.**
What **was** the security guard **doing** She **was sitting** in a chair	**while**	you **were waiting** for the elevator? I **was waiting** for the elevator.

accomplice
automatic
automatically
by (near)
disk drive
diskette
drinking fountain
elderly
elevator
fingerprint
guy
lens cover
light switch
murder
original

painting
report
restroom
screen
select
statue
valuable
VCR
video
volume
wheelchair
while

Hey (you)!
wait a minute
You're kidding!

VERBS

aim
be worth
come [came/come]
eject
enter
focus
go [went/gone] out (lights)
lean
litter
park
place
pretend
record
run [ran/run]
shoot [shot/shot]
steal [stole/stolen]
trip
win [won/won]
wind [wound/wound]

SEPARABLE TWO-WORD VERBS*

pick up
pull down
put [put/put] in
put on
take [took/taken] off
take out
try out
turn off (on)
turn up (down)
write [wrote/written] down

*Complete list is on page 127.

ASKING FOR AND GIVING INSTRUCTIONS

How does this copy machine work?
　　You turn the machine on here. Then you place the original here.

REQUESTING, VERIFYING, AND RESTATING

Would you turn the VCR on, please?
　　The VCR?
Yes. Turn it on, please.

MAKING AND REJECTING SUGGESTIONS

Let's have a cigarette.
　　There's no smoking in the theater.

GIVING REASONS

Why didn't you answer the phone?
　　I was so busy that I didn't hear it.

GIVING OPINIONS

I don't think Roberto has a lot of experience with cameras because he forgot to put the film in.

I believe that Pravit and his wife work hard because Pravit always works around the house and San works at the museum.

FINDING OUT WHERE PEOPLE WERE AND WHAT THEY WERE DOING

Where were you at 7:00 last night?
　　I was at home.
What were you doing?
　　I was studying. While I was studying, San was working.
Was Pravit washing his car at 4:00 yesterday afternoon?
　　Yes, he was.
　　No, he wasn't.

TALKING ABOUT WHAT HAPPENED

What can you tell me about the robbery?
　　When the lights went out, the security guard was sitting in a
　　chair. Now she is standing by the light switch.

ASKING FOR CONFIRMATION

The painting cost $200,000, didn't it?
　　No, it didn't. It cost $250,000.
Horton was sitting in a wheelchair, wasn't he?
　　Yes, he was.

Did you hurt yourself?

Listen as you read the conversation. Find out the meaning of the words
you don't understand. 🔊

Olga:	Were you able to fix the lawn mower?
Eddie:	No, so I couldn't mow the lawn.
Olga:	Ouch!
Eddie:	What's the matter? Did you hurt yourself?
Olga:	I cut myself.
Eddie:	Do you want some help?
Olga:	No. I'm all right. I can finish it myself. Why don't you help your sister clean the living room? There are records and books everywhere.
Eddie:	Those are all Isabel's things. Anyway, she doesn't want any help.
Olga:	Well, check with your father. I think he's ready to paint the kitchen, and it's too big for him to paint alone.
Eddie:	Do I have to?
Olga:	Yes, you have to. He won't be able to do it by himself. It'll take too long.

Respond to the statements with *That's right, That's wrong,* or *It doesn't say.* Correct the statements that are wrong.

1. Eddie fixed the lawn mower.
2. Eddie didn't mow the lawn.
3. Eddie likes mowing the lawn.
4. Olga cut her hand badly.
5. Isabel doesn't want Eddie's help.
6. Eddie's father loves to paint.
7. The kitchen is big.
8. Eddie doesn't like to paint.

Listen to and look at the example. Then listen and complete the other sentences with the correct form of the verb *be.*

> I **wasn't** able to fix the lawn mower, so I couldn't mow the lawn.

1. I _____ able to put up the window shades, but I couldn't put the curtains up.
2. They _____ able to meet us after the football game, so we'll tell them the news then.
3. She _____ able to help clean the basement because she won't be here when you're ready to begin.
4. He _____ able to play baseball with us this afternoon. He has to do some chores around the house.
5. If they _____ able to fix the car today, they can fix it tomorrow.
6. They _____ able to get here on time, so we began without them.

Complete the conversation between Eddie and his father. Use the correct tense of *be able to* and the verb in parentheses. Then listen and check your answers.

> **Dad:** **Were you able to fix** the lawn mower, Eddie?

Eddie: No, so I (¹mow) _____ the lawn until tomorrow.

Dad: (²help) _____ you _____ me with the kitchen, then? I want to start painting it in a few minutes.

Eddie: Gee, Dad, I have to clean the basement for Mom first.

Dad: Well, (³paint) _____ you _____ later?

Eddie: Yeah. I (⁴help) _____ you after lunch.

Dad: By the way, (⁵ find) _____ you _____ that tie you borrowed last night?

Eddie: Uh . . . no. If I (⁶not find) _____ it, I'll buy you a new one. OK?

Dad: It was my favorite tie.

Eddie: I know, Dad. I've looked everywhere, and I (⁷not find) _____ it. But I'll keep looking.

Refer to exercise 3 and complete this chart.

Present	Present Perfect	Past	Future
can		could	can
is able to are able to		was able to were able to	

Now read the conversation in exercise 3 and substitute *can* and *could*, if possible.

Talk to your classmates. Find someone who . . .

1. was able to do exercise 4 without any mistakes.

> **A:** *Were* **you able to** *do exercise 4 without any mistakes?*
> **B:** **Yes, I** *was.*   (**No, I** *wasn't.*)

2. is able to speak English well.
3. has been able to learn English very quickly.
4. will be able to continue studying after this class ends.
5. will be able to use English at work someday.
6. is able to fix things (lawn mowers, radios, etc.).

Look at and listen to the example and complete each conversation with the appropriate reflexive pronoun from the list. After you finish, listen to each exchange.

myself	ourselves
yourself	yourselves
himself	themselves
herself	
itself	

> **A:** Did she hurt **herself**?
> **B:** Yes. She burned **herself**.

1. A: Did you make a sandwich for Eddie?
   B: No, he made one for _____ .

2. A: What are you writing about?
   B: I'm writing about _____ .

3. A: Eddie and Isabel are having fun.
   B: Yes. They're really enjoying _____ .

4. A: That little dog hurt its foot.
   B: Don't worry. It'll take care of _____.

5. A: Olga played tennis very well.
   B: Yes. She must feel good about _____ .

6. A: Let's go out to dinner tonight.
   B: Yes. Let's enjoy _____ tonight.

7. A: We saw a wonderful movie.
   B: I'm glad you enjoyed _____ .

8. A: Did you burn ____?
   B: No, we're all right.

9. A: Did you hurt yourself?
   B: Yes. I cut _____.

10. A: Did she eat those cookies?
    B: Yes. She ate them all _____.

Complete these sentences. Use reflexive pronouns for emphasis.

> I don't need any help. I can finish it **myself**.
> He can't paint the kitchen alone. He won't be able to do it by **himself**.

1. No one helped Isabel with her homework. She did it _____ .
2. I like living alone. I enjoy being by _____ .
3. It was a nice party. Lynn and Keiko planned it _____ .
4. We don't like being alone. We're bored when we're by _____ .
5. Eddie is good at repairing things, so he fixed the lawn mower _____ .

After you check your answers, ask and answer these questions about yourselves.

6. Who do you live with?
7. Who made your breakfast this morning?
8. Who helped you do your homework last night?
9. Who did you come to school with today?

Look at the answers to the questions and combine the sentences. Then listen and check your answers. 🖭

> **A:** Why is everyone helping him?
> **B:** Because the kitchen is very big. He can't paint it alone.
> Because the kitchen is **too big to paint** alone.
>
> **A:** Why did you turn off the TV?
> **B:** Because I was very tired. I didn't watch the movie.
> Because I was **too tired to watch** the movie.

1. A: Why did you stop working?
   B: Because the work is hard. I can't do the work by myself.

2. A: Why has she gone home already?
   B: Because she was very tired. She couldn't stay and play another game.

3. A: Why is he leaving?
   B: Because he's very impatient. He won't wait for us.

4. A: Where have you been?
   B: I've been sick. I haven't been able to come to school.

5. A: What did they say when you gave them the gift?
   B: They were very surprised. They didn't say anything.

6. A: How did you hit the truck?
   B: We were driving very fast. We couldn't stop.

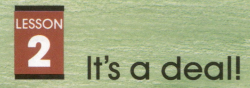

LESSON 2 It's a deal!

Listen as you read the conversation. Find out the meaning of the words you don't understand. 🔲

Sandy: Have you finished helping your parents?

Isabel: I finished cleaning the living room a little while ago, but I haven't cleaned my bedroom yet. Housework is exhausting. I'm exhausted.

Sandy: I know what you mean. I hate doing chores around the house. Do you think you'll be finished soon?

Isabel: I should be done in about an hour.

Sandy: Have you looked at Monday's homework yet?

Isabel: I did the English homework last night, but I haven't started my math yet. I don't understand it.

Sandy: Me neither. Why don't we do it together this afternoon? We can help each other figure it out.

Isabel: OK. Then we can cut each other's hair.

Sandy: Great.

Isabel: By the way, if you lend your blue sweater to me, I'll lend you my new Whitney Houston album.

Sandy: It's a deal. See you in a little while.

Read the conversation on page 66 again. Then choose the right explanation (a–f) for the phrases (1–6).

1. I finished cleaning the living room *a little while* ago.
2. I should be *done* in about an hour.
3. *Me neither.*
4. *We can help each other* figure it out.
5. Then *we can cut each other's hair.*
6. *It's a deal.*

a. I don't either.
b. You can help me, and I can help you.
c. a short time
d. I can cut your hair, and you can cut mine.
e. I agree.
f. finished

Complete the conversation with the words in parentheses. Use the correct tense of the verbs: the present perfect, the simple past, or the present continuous. Then listen and check your answers.

> **Olga:** Isabel, **have you finished** cleaning the living room yet?
> **Isabel:** Yes. **I finished** a little while ago.
> **Olga: Have you cleaned** your bedroom?
> **Isabel:** No. **I'm doing** it now.

Olga: Eddie, (**1**. you/repair) the lawn mower yet?
Eddie: Yes. (**2**. I/fix) it yesterday.
Olga: (**3**. you/mow) the lawn?
Eddie: (**4**. I/just/finish) mowing it.
Olga: Hector, (**5**. you/paint) the kitchen?
Hector: (**6**. I/already/finish) the walls.
Olga: (**7**. you/start) the cupboards yet?
Hector: (**8**. I/paint) them now.
Olga: (**9**. you/already/put up) the new blinds?
Eddie: Yes, but (**10**. I/not/wash) the windows yet.
   I can't wash them right now because
   (**11**. I/cut) my hand a few minutes ago.

> **What about you?**
> Have you and your classmates finished exercise 1?
> Have you and your classmates done exercise 2?
> Have you and your classmates started exercise 3 yet?

Find out the meaning of the verbs you don't know and complete the chart.

Verb	Present Participle	Past Participle
exhaust	exhausting	exhausted
interest		
bore	boring	
excite		excited
confuse	confusing	
surprise		
embarrass		

Now look at the pictures and decide what the people are thinking. Use the words in the chart.

Housework exhausts me. **It's exhausting. I'm exhausted.**

1. Art interests me.
   It _____ .

2. This book bores me.
   I _____ .

3. Soccer excites me.
   It _____ .

4. This map confuses
   me. I _____ .

5. This party surprises
   me. I _____ .

6. This embarrasses
   me. It _____ .

Make two sentences using the words in parentheses. The list of verbs in the grammar summary on page 74 will tell you if you should use *to* or *for*.

I'll lend (my blue sweater/you).

  a. I'll lend **my blue sweater to you**.

  b. I'll lend **you my blue sweater**.

I'll get (it/you) in a minute.

  a. I'll get **it for you** in a minute.

  b. _____

1. What am I going to do? I haven't found (a gift/my father yet).
   a. _____
   b. _____

2. I sent (a book/him) for his birthday last year.
   a. _____
   b. _____

3. Unfortunately, I gave (a boring one/him).
   a. _____
   b. _____

4. He read (a page/me), and it was terrible.
   a. _____
   b. _____

5. My boyfriend was cooking (dinner/me).
   a. _____
   b. _____

6. I wanted to show (my appreciation/him).
   a. _____
   b. _____

7. So I took (a box of candy/him).
   a. _____
   b. _____

8. While he wasn't looking, I left (it on the table/him).
   a. _____
   b. _____

9. I used to tell (stories/my little brother).
   a. _____
   b. _____

10. I used to teach (songs/him), too.
    a. _____
    b. _____

11. Now he is at the university, and I write (letters/him).
    a. _____
    b. _____

12. And sometimes I buy (gifts/him).
    a. _____
    b. _____

Isabel is at Sandy's house. Listen and complete the conversation. 🔲

Sandy: Are you hungry?
Isabel: Yeah. I haven't had lunch yet.
¹_____?
Sandy: Sure. ²_____ .
Isabel: ³_____?
Sandy: Yeah. ⁴_____?
Isabel: Sure. Let me get it.
Sandy: Oh, ⁵_____? I can't find mine.
Isabel: Here. This sandwich is delicious.
Sandy: Thanks.
Isabel: ⁶_____? Thanks.

Work with a partner and practice making requests and suggestions. Use the ideas in the list or your own ideas. Listen to the examples. 🔲

lend/your pen   get/something to drink
show/your homework   pass/the salt and pepper
make/something to eat your own ideas

1. Make a request.

> **A: Could you** *lend me your pen*?
> **B: Sure. I'll** *lend it to you* **in a minute.**

2. Make a suggestion.

> **A: If you** *show me your homework*, **I'll** *lend you my new cassettes*.
> **B: It's a deal.**

Make different sentences with *each other* and *each other's*.

> I can help you figure it out, and you can help me.
> We can help **each other** figure it out.
>
> You can cut my hair, and I can cut yours.
> We can cut **each other's** hair.

1. Sometimes I use my father's car, and sometimes he uses mine.
   Sometimes my father and I use _____ .

2. Is Gina going to help Frank with the housework, and is Frank going to help Gina?
   Are Gina and Frank going to help _____ ?

3. He bought her a sweater for her birthday, and she bought him one for his. They bought _____ sweaters.

4. I always share my cassettes with my sister, and she always shares her cassettes with me.
   We always share _____ .

5. Did you remember his name, and did he remember yours?
   Did you remember _____ ?

6. I might help her with her homework, and she might help me with mine.
   We might help _____ .

Chores and leisure time

CONDOMINIUMS FIT TODAY'S LIFE STYLE

(1) Many people have started living in condominium homes, houses and apartments that share the same walls and the same services. Single people, young families, and the elderly buy condominiums, or "condos," for several reasons. Also, condos are often cheaper than traditional individual houses.

(2) Condominiums fit today's life style. A lot of people aren't interested in working in gardens, mowing lawns, and doing other chores around the house in the evenings and on the weekends. They don't want these responsibilities. When they aren't at work, they want to be able to travel, play sports, and enjoy other leisure-time activities. When they are at home, they want to relax and enjoy themselves.

A traditional house

(3) Of course, people still have to clean and paint the inside of their homes, but they don't have to worry about cleaning or painting the outside. And they don't have to mow the lawn or find someone to pick up the garbage. In a condo, full-or part-time workers take care of these services.

(4) The elderly often like living in condos because they aren't able to take care of traditional houses and lawns. Also, they enjoy having friends nearby—for social reasons and for security. Security is another good reason for living in a condominium. People live in groups of three, four, or more homes. Also, if no one is at home, there are always several neighbors who can keep their eyes on the empty house.

Today's condominium

EXERCISE 1

Without using a dictionary or discussing the vocabulary, read the article to yourself and answer the questions.

1. Which two paragraphs discuss *services*?
2. Which paragraph mentions *leisure-time activities*?
3. Which paragraph discusses *security*?

Now decide if these items are (1) services, (2) leisure-time activities, or (3) security.

a. traveling __2__

b. having neighbors who can watch your house ____

c. playing sports ____

d. reading ____

e. mowing someone's lawn ____

f. having a security guard near your house ____

g. painting the outside of someone's house ____

h. feeling safe at home ____

i. picking up someone's garbage ____

j. cleaning someone's swimming pool ____

k. going to a movie ____

Work with a group and choose the best answer.

1. *Life style* in the title and in paragraph 2 means
   a. how people live.
   b. how people work and play.
   c. both a and b.

2. *Little upkeep* in paragraph 1 means
   a. people have only a few leisure-time activities.
   b. people don't have to take care of things—for example, the lawn or the garbage.
   c. both a and b.

3. Examples of *the inside* in paragraph 3 are
   a. the lawn, the garden, and the garage.
   b. the bedrooms, the living room, and the kitchen.
   c. both a and b.

4. Examples of *social reasons* in paragraph 4 are
   a. conversations, dinner, and parties.
   b. feeling safe and having neighbors who will keep their eyes on your home.
   c. both a and b.

Listen and then choose the correct words in parentheses.

1. The man (liked/didn't like) the movie.
2. He (enjoyed/didn't enjoy) himself.
3. He went to the movie (alone/with his girlfriend).
4. The woman and her husband (liked/didn't like) the museum.
5. They were (fascinated by/disappointed with) the paintings.
6. The woman and her husband went (by themselves/with some friends).
7. The restaurant was (wonderful/terrible).
8. The man (enjoyed himself/was disappointed).
9. He went to the restaurant (alone/with his girlfriend).

Complete this chart with a classmate's answers.

Questions	Answers
What was the last movie you saw?	**Rain Man**
What was the last museum you visited?	
What was the last concert you went to?	
What was the last restaurant you ate in?	

Now practice this conversation. Use the answers from the chart. Listen to the examples.

A: **How was** *Rain Man*?
B: **I liked it. The** *story (paintings, music, food) was very interesting.*
A: **I'm glad you enjoyed yourself.**

OR

B: **I didn't like it. The** *story wasn't very interesting.*
A: **I'm sorry you were disappointed.**

B: **Me, too.**
A: **Who did you go with?**
B: **I went** *by myself* (with Sandy).

Talk to your classmates and take notes. Try to find two people who . . .

Now report your findings to the class like this:

1. enjoy themselves in this city.
2. are bored here.
3. live by themselves.
4. like doing chores around the house.
5. hate doing chores around the house.
6. live near each other.
7. come to school together.
8. help each other with their English homework.
9. hurt themselves recently while they were doing a chore.
10. hurt themselves recently during a leisure-time activity.

Glen and Linda Sue enjoy themselves here.
No one is bored here.
The teacher lives by himself.

Paragraphs 2 and 4 in this letter are not divided into appropriate sentences.
Rewrite the paragraphs.

Dear Alan,

I'm still in Dallas. I can't believe that I've already been here for two years. I guess time passes very quickly when you're enjoying yourself.

I still live by myself and I still live in the same house it's not a very exciting house, but it's mine and there isn't much upkeep you know that I hate doing chores!

I've been at the Language Institute for a year and a half. I can speak English pretty well now and I think I'll be able to get a good job because of it. I'll probably study here for six more months although I have thought about staying another year.

My best friend and I live near each other we go to school together and help each other with our homework we also spend a lot of our free time together we like going swimming and going to restaurants.

Well, I guess that's everything. Oh, I almost forgot. While I was painting the outside of my house last week, I fell and broke my arm. Luckily, it's my left arm so I'm able to write this letter!

Write soon.

Your friend,
Luis

Now write a letter and bring a friend up to date. Use the model above as an example.

REVIEW: THE PRESENT PERFECT, THE SIMPLE PAST, AND THE PRESENT CONTINUOUS

Have you **finished** cleaning the living room yet?
   Yes, I **finished** a little while ago.
Have you **cleaned** your bedroom?
   No. **I'm doing** it now.

BE ABLE TO

Statements

I	'm able to		
He	was able to	fix	it.
They	haven't been able to		

Yes/No Questions

Are	you		able to		
Was	he		able to	fix	it?
Have	they	been able to			

Short Answers

	I am.			I'm not.
Yes,	I was.	No,		I wasn't.
	I have.			I haven't.

REFLEXIVE PRONOUNS

I		myself.
You		yourself.
He		himself.
She	hurt	herself.
It		itself.
We		ourselves.
You		yourselves.
They		themselves.

I can finish it **myself.**
He won't be able to do it by **himself.**

RECIPROCAL PRONOUNS

We can help **each other** figure it out.
We can cut **each other's** hair.

TOO ... TO

The kitchen is **too** big **to** paint by himself.

PRESENT AND PAST PARTICIPLES AS ADJECTIVES

Housework exhausts me. It's **exhausting.** I'm **exhausted.**

VERBS + OBJECTS + *TO*

give	read	teach
lend	send	tell
pass	show	write
	take	

VERBS + OBJECTS + *FOR*

buy	get
cook	leave
find	make

I'll	lend	you my sweater.	
		my sweater	to you.
		it	

I'll	get	you my sweater.	
		my sweater	for you.
		it	

appreciation
condominium
course
housework
inside
lawn
lawn mower
leisure
life style
luckily
service
share
social
someday
unfortunately
upkeep

a little while
by the way
Gee.
Me neither.
Ouch!

REFLEXIVE PRONOUNS

myself   ourselves
yourself   yourselves
herself   themselves
himself
itself

VOCABULARY

VERBS

be able to
be careful
borrow
burn
do [did/done] chores
go out (to a place)
hurt [hurt/hurt]
lend [lent/lent]
mow
pass
share

ADJECTIVES FROM VERBS

bore	bored/boring
confuse	confused/
	confusing
disappoint	disappointed/
	disappointing
do	done
embarrass	embarrassed/
	embarrassing
excite	excited/exciting
exhaust	exhausted/
	exhausting
fascinate	fascinated/
	fascinating
finish	finished
interest	interested/
	interesting
surprise	surprised/
	surprising

COMMUNICATION SUMMARY

GIVING REASONS

Why is everyone helping you?
  Because the kitchen is too big to paint alone.

GIVING OPINIONS

The story wasn't very interesting.
This map is confusing.

TALKING ABOUT ABILITY

Are you able to fix things?
  Yes, I am.
Were you able to do exercise 5 without any mistakes?
  No, I wasn't.

TALKING ABOUT WHAT YOU HAVE DONE

Have you finished exercise 1 yet?
  Yes, we have. We finished it a few minutes ago.
Have you done exercise 2?
  No. We're doing it now.

EXPRESSING RECIPROCAL RELATIONSHIPS

We can help **each other** figure it out.
Let's cut **each other's** hair.

MAKING SUGGESTIONS

If you help me with my homework, I'll lend you my new record.
  It's a deal.

ASKING FOR PERSONAL INFORMATION

Who do you live with?
  I live by myself.
Who helped you do your homework?
  No one. I did it myself.
Who did you come to school with?
  I walked with Sandy.
Did you hurt yourself?
  Yes. I cut myself.

TALKING ABOUT LEISURE-TIME ACTIVITIES

How was *Rain Man*?
  I liked it. The story was very interesting.
I'm glad you enjoyed yourself.

MAKING REQUESTS

Could you lend me your pen?
  Sure. I'll lend it to you in a minute.

SAYING HOW YOU FEEL

I'm exhausted.
I was disappointed.

UNIT 7

LESSON 1

It smells delicious!

Listen as you read the conversation. Find out the meaning of the words you don't understand.

Oscar: What are you making, Lucy? It smells delicious!

Pierre: Yes, it smells like cinnamon and nutmeg. What is it?

Lucy: It's a carrot cake.

Oscar: What's in it?

Lucy: Eggs, oil, sugar, flour, carrots, raisins, nuts, and spices.

Pierre: It sounds terrific. Do you think it tastes good, Oscar?

Oscar: I don't know, but it sure looks good.

Lucy: All right, you guys. You can have a piece when I'm finished. But you'll have to wait. I have to go to the store. I don't have enough sugar for the frosting.

Pierre: How much do you need?

Lucy: I've only got half a cup, and I need a cup.

Pierre: I'll be right back. I think I've got some extra sugar in the cupboard.

76

Refer to the conversation on page 76 again and then answer these questions.

1. What's in a carrot cake?
2. Two spices are mentioned in the conversation. What are they?
3. Do you think Oscar and Pierre would like some cake? Why do you think so?

4. Has Lucy finished making the cake?
5. What else does she have to do?
6. Do you think Pierre lives near Lucy? Why do you think so?

Choose the sentence that matches the picture.

1. a. She looks great!
   b. She looks awful!

2. a. She looks great!
   b. She looks awful!

3. a. It smells terrible!
   b. It smells wonderful!

4. a. It smells terrible!
   b. It smells wonderful!

5. a. It tastes good!
   b. It tastes bad!

6. a. It tastes good!
   b. It tastes bad!

7. a. The band sounds terrible!
   b. The band sounds terrific!

8. a. The band sounds terrible!
   b. The band sounds terrific!

9. a. It feels nice!
   b. It feels awful!

10. a. It feels nice!
    b. It feels awful!

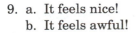

UNIT 7   77

First look at the pictures and guess what the things are.

It **looks like** a cat.

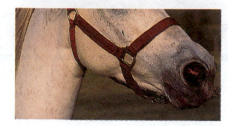

1. _____

2. _____

3. _____

4. _____

5. _____

6. _____

Now listen and write what you hear. Listen to the example.

It **sounds like** a cat.

a. _____ d. _____
b. _____ e. _____
c. _____ f. _____

After you check your answers, match them with the pictures above.

Lucy is in a supermarket. First practice the conversation. Then change *have* to *have got*. Use contractions *('ve/haven't)* if possible.

> Lucy: **Excuse me,** *do you have* **any sugar? I looked, but I couldn't find any.**
> Manager: **I'm sorry. We're out of sugar.**
> Lucy: *Do you have* **any cinnamon? I couldn't find that either.**
> Manager: **I'm sure** *we have* **cinnamon.**
> Lucy: **I looked, but I didn't see it. I didn't see any nutmeg either.**
> Manager: **Let me check . . . . You were right. We** *don't have* **any cinnamon, but** *we have* **nutmeg.**

Now listen to the conversation. 🔲

Look at Lucy's and Pierre's shopping lists. They crossed out the things the store is out of. Practice the conversation with the items in each list. 📼

A: **Have you got any** *sugar*?
B: **No. I'm sorry. We're out of** *sugar*.
A: **Have you got any** *cinnamon*?
B: **No. We haven't got any** *cinnamon* **either.**
A: **How about** *nutmeg*?
B: **Yes. I'm sure we've got** *nutmeg*.

Now practice the conversation with three items from your own list.

Lucy wanted to make another carrot cake. Why did she go to the supermarket? Look at the recipe and make sentences like this:

Lucy had only half a cup of sugar. She didn't have **enough** sugar. She needed **a cup**.

CARROT CAKE

4 eggs
1½ cups oil
1 cup sugar
2 cups flour
2 teaspoons baking soda
2 teaspoons cinnamon

½ teaspoon nutmeg
¼ teaspoon salt
2 cups shredded carrots
1 cup raisins
½ cup chopped walnuts
1 teaspoon vanilla

1. Lucy had only one teaspoon of cinnamon.
2. She had only a little nutmeg.
3. She had only two eggs.

4. She had only a few walnuts.
5. She had only one carrot.
6. She had only one cup of oil.

Gina wanted to try making Lucy's carrot cake. At home she had 1 cup of flour, 4 cups of sugar, 3 eggs, 2 cups of walnuts, ½ cup of raisins, and 1 cup of oil. Ask questions about Gina. Check the recipe in exercise 6 before you answer. Listen to the examples. 📼

A: **Did she have enough** *flour*?
B: **No, she didn't.**

A: **Did she have enough** *sugar*?
B: **Yes, she had plenty of** *sugar*.
   (Yes, she did.)

What an awful cake!

Listen as you read the conversation. Find out the meaning of the words you don't understand. 🔊

Pierre: What an awful cake! And what terrible frosting!
Oscar: Yeah. Wasn't it bad?
Pierre: Yes, it was. I don't think it baked long enough, and the frosting was too sweet.
Oscar: Yeah, it was so sweet I couldn't finish eating it.
Pierre: I guess I've had enough sugar to last a year.
Oscar: I guess you have! Didn't you have a second piece?
Pierre: Yeah. I was being polite.
Oscar: How could you eat it?
Pierre: I kept drinking a lot of coffee with it.
Oscar: Could you hold this for a second? I need a drink. I still taste it.

Choose the correct explanation for the words and phrases in the conversation on page 80.

1. *What an awful cake!*
2. *Wasn't it bad?*
3. I don't think it baked *long enough.*
4. *I've had enough sugar to last a year.*
5. *Didn't you have a second piece?*
6. *Could you* hold this for a second?
7. I *still* taste it.

a. continue to
b. That cake was terrible!
c. Would you
d. for enough time
e. I don't need to eat sugar for a year.
f. It was bad, wasn't it?
g. You had a second piece, didn't you?

Look at the pictures and tell what the people are saying.

What an awful sandwich!

What terrible frosting!

1. _____ sweet apple!

2. _____ sour oranges!

3. _____ delicious soup!

4. _____ beautiful day!

5. _____ awful weather!

6. Say what you think.

Ask the questions a different way. Give your own answers.

> **A:** Lucy's cake was terrible, **wasn't it?**
> **Wasn't** Lucy's cake terrible?
> **B:** Yes, it was. (No, it wasn't.)

1. Lucy is a good cook, isn't she?
2. Lucy puts carrots in her cake, doesn't she?
3. Oscar and Pierre liked her cake, didn't they?
4. Pierre was able to eat a second piece, wasn't he?
5. They'll look forward to having Lucy's cake again, won't they?
6. YOU have had carrot cake before, haven't you?

Listen and complete the conversations.

1. A: Lucy's cake was very sweet.
   B: But _____ ? I thought you did.
   A: Yes, I did. I was being polite.

2. A: They didn't have enough sugar for the recipe.
   B: _____ ?
   A: No, they didn't. They didn't make the cake.

3. A: Victor bought a new car.
   B: Oh, really? _____ ?
   A: Yes, it looks very nice.

4. A: My class starts at 6:30.
   B: It's already 6:25. _____ ?
   A: Yes, but the teacher is always late.

5. A: Would you like to go see *Rain Man*?
   B: _____ ? I thought you went last week.
   A: I did, but I want to see it again.

6. A: _____ ? I think I've seen you there.
   B: Yes, I do.
   A: I thought so.

After you check your answers, decide if the speaker in each conversation asks for *more information* or for *confirmation*. Look at the examples.

1. In number 1, the speaker asks for confirmation.
2. In number 2, the speaker asks for more information.
3. _____
4. _____
5. _____
6. _____

Look at what each person is saying. Then tell the person's complete thought. Use your imagination.

It was **too** sour **to eat.**

This sweater is **so** big **I can't wear it.**

1. _____

2. _____

3. _____

4. _____

5. _____

6. _____

Look at each picture in exercise 5 and say what the problem is. Listen to the examples. 📼

The apple was (sour/sweet).

The apple was too sour. It wasn't sweet **enough** to eat.

The sweater is (big/small).

The sweater is too big. It isn't small **enough** to wear.

1. The box is (heavy/light).
2. It's (dark/light).
3. The pants are (short/long).
4. They'll be (late/early).

5. It has been (hot/cool).
6. The homework was (hard/easy).

Make requests with *Would you . . .* , *Could you . . .* , or *Could I . . . .* Listen to the examples. 📼

lend me your notebook

A: Would (Could) you *lend me your notebook,* **please?**
B: Sure. (I'm sorry. I don't have it.)

borrow a pencil

A: Could I *borrow a pencil,* **please?**
B: Sure. (I'm sorry. I don't have one.)

1. lend me a pen
2. borrow a piece of paper
3. see your English book
4. show me your homework

5. see your notebook
6. have a piece of gum
7. give me a dollar
8. Make your own request.

Did you know that . . . ?

EXERCISE 1

Read the article. Find the words in the article with numbers next to them. What do these words refer to?

[1]*it* refers to __**Texas**__ .

[2]*He* refers to _____ .

[3]*It* refers to _____ .

[4]*this kind of meal* refers to _____ .

[5]*they* refers to _____ .

[6]*they* refers to _____ .

[7]*it* refers to _____ .

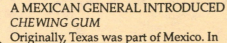

DID YOU KNOW THAT ...?

A MEXICAN GENERAL INTRODUCED *CHEWING GUM*

Originally, Texas was part of Mexico. In 1836, the Texans defeated Mexican General Antonio Lopez de Santa Anna and Texas became independent. In 1845, [1]it became a state. And what happened to General Santa Anna? Santa Anna entered the United States and moved to New York. [2]He took one of his favorite habits with him – chewing chicle. Chicle came from a Mexican tree. [3]It looked and felt like rubber. It probably tasted like rubber, too. In New York, Santa Anna introduced chicle to a photographer and inventor, Thomas Adams. Adams's "gum" went on sale in a New Jersey drugstore in 1871. Today, gum isn't made from chicle. It's made from a kind of plastic.

A BRITISH FOREIGN SECRETARY INTRODUCED THE *SANDWICH*

John Montagu, the fourth Earl of Sandwich, was a gambler. He refused to leave the gambling tables for meals. While he was gambling, he sometimes ordered sliced meat and cheese between pieces of bread so he could eat with one hand and play with the other. One day in 1762, when he was 44 years old and the British foreign secretary, he spent 24 hours at the gambling tables. As usual, he ordered his meals between slices of bread — and people started calling [4]this kind of meal a "sandwich."

AN AMERICAN INDIAN INVENTED *POTATO CHIPS*

In the summer of 1853, a chef at a hotel in Saratoga Springs, New York, received a complaint from one of the guests in the hotel restraurant. The chef was an American Indian named George Crum. Two times the guest said he did not like Crum's French fries because [5]they were too thick. The third time, Crum got angry and cut the potatoes so thin that they didn't look like French fries at all. Crum was surprised. The guest loved the new kind of potatoes, and soon other guests at the hotel wanted them, too. And so potato chips were born — by accident.

ICE CREAM ORIGINATED IN CHINA

About 4,000 years ago, the Chinese began using the milk from their farm animals. Sometimes [6]they mixed milk with rice and spices and then cooled [7]it in the snow. This "milk ice" was an important food for the rich. Later, the Chinese added fruit and fruit juices to snow or to milk. By the thirteenth century, many kinds of iced desserts were available on the streets of Peking.

Source: Charles Panati, *Extraordinary Origins of Everyday Things*, Perennial Library (Harper & Row, 1987), pp. 388-89, 400, 416-21.

How much do you remember? Complete these summaries. Scan the article in exercise 1 if you need help.

CHEWING GUM

Originally, people made chewing gum from _____ . Chicle came from a Mexican _____ . Chicle looked and felt like _____ . A Mexican general _____ chicle to the United States.

POTATO CHIPS

Potato chips originated in _____ in 1853. A chef made them by _____ when a guest said the chef's French fries were too _____ . The chef cut the _____ so thin that they didn't _____ French fries at all.

THE SANDWICH

Originally, a sandwich was _____ meat and cheese between pieces of _____ . The sandwich got its name in the _____ century from the fourth earl of _____ . The Earl of Sandwich ordered "sandwiches" so he could _____ with one hand and gamble with the _____ .

ICE CREAM

Answer these four questions and write your own summary: Where did ice cream originate? When did it originate? At first, it was a mixture of what? Was this first "ice cream" an important food for anyone?

In groups or with the class, make a survey.

1. What are the favorite "snacks" in your country? That is, what do people like to eat between meals, at the movies, and during their leisure time? Make a list.
2. Do you know which snacks on the list originated in your country? Do you know where the others came from?
3. From the list, what is your own favorite snack? What don't you like at all? Give reasons for your choices like this:

Favorite Snacks in (Country)		
Snack	Originated in *my country*	Originated in *another country*
1.		
2.		
3.		
4.		

I like *ice cream* **because** *I like sweet things.*
I hate *potato chips* **because** *they're too salty.*
I don't like *lemonade* **because** *it's so sour.*

Two friends are talking on the phone. One is giving the other her recipe for carrot cake. Listen and complete the recipe. 🔲

2 teaspoons baking soda
2 teaspoons cinnamon

½ cup chopped walnuts
1 teaspoon vanilla

Preheat the oven to **1**____. Grease two 9-inch **2**____ cake pans or one **3**____ by 13-inch pan. With an electric mixer, **4**____ the eggs, oil, and **5**____. With the mixer on **6**____, add the flour, baking soda, **7**____, and salt. With a **8**____, stir in the carrots, **9**____, walnuts, and vanilla. Pour **10**____ mixture into the pans. **11**____ for 35 minutes or **12**____ a toothpick comes out **13**____. Cool for 10 minutes, **14**____ remove the cake from the **15**____.

EXERCISE 5

Choose one of these activities. Write your recipe or summary.

1. Pretend an international visitor has asked you for one of your favorite recipes. Write down the recipe. If possible, also make your favorite recipe and bring a sample to class.
2. Write a summary about one of your favorite **snacks** or national foods. Follow the models in exercise 2.

EXERCISE 6

Pretend that your partner is cooking or baking something and practice the conversation. Talk about your own favorite recipes. Listen to the example. 🔲

A: What smells so good?
B: It's *a carrot cake.*
A: What's in it?
B: *Eggs, oil, sugar, flour, carrots, raisins, nuts, and spices.*
A: It sounds terrific.
B: I hope it tastes *good.*

GRAMMAR SUMMARY

REVIEW: *HAVE GOT*

Have you **got** any sugar?
I'm sure we**'ve got** nutmeg.
We **haven't got** any cinnamon either.

REVIEW: *TOO AND SO*

It's **too** sweet. I can't eat it.
It was **too** sweet to eat.
This sweater is **so** big I can't wear it.

REVIEW: REQUESTS WITH *WOULD* **AND** *COULD*

Would you lend me your notebook, please?
Could you lend me your notebook, please?
Could I borrow a pencil, please?

LOOK, FEEL, SOUND, SMELL, **AND**
TASTE **+ ADJECTIVE**

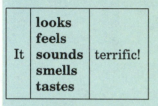

It	**looks** **feels** **sounds** **smells** **tastes**	terrific!

LOOK, FEEL, SOUND, SMELL, **AND**
TASTE **+** *LIKE* **+ NOUN**

	looks		a dog.
	feels		rubber.
It	**sounds**	like	a cat.
	smells		cinnamon.
	tastes		chocolate.

REVIEW: *ENOUGH*

She didn't have **enough** sugar.
The sweater is too small. It isn't big **enough** to wear.

WHAT (A/AN)

What	**an** awful cake! sour oranges! terrible frosting!

NEGATIVE YES/NO QUESTIONS

Isn't Lucy a good cook?
Wasn't Lucy's cake terrible?
Don't you live in Dallas?
Didn't you have a second piece?
Won't you be late?
Haven't you seen that movie already?

VOCABULARY

British
century
(chewing) gum
confirmation
degree (°)
earl
gambler
general
guest
habit
iced
independent
inventor
lately
light (not dark)
like (conjunction)
part of
plastic
plenty of
round
rubber
speaker
thick

as usual
by accident
I'll be right back.

FOOD AND COOKING

carrot
chopped
cinnamon
electric mixer
frosting
fruit
lemonade
nutmeg
potato chip
raisin
salty
shredded
sliced
snack
sour
spice
spoon
sweet
teaspoon

VOCABULARY

VERBS

be made from
be out of
beat [beat/beaten]
defeat
gamble
go on sale
grease
hold [held/held]
last
originate
pour
smell
sound
taste

COMMUNICATION SUMMARY

ASKING ABOUT AVAILABILITY

Have you got any sugar?
   No. I'm sorry. We're out of sugar.
Have you got any cinnamon?
   No. We haven't got any cinnamon either.
How about nutmeg?
   Yes. I'm sure we've got nutmeg.

Did she have enough flour?
   Yes. She had plenty of flour.

ASKING FOR CONFIRMATION

Isn't Lucy a good cook?
   Yes, she is.
Don't you live in Dallas?
   Yes, I do.
Wasn't Lucy's cake terrible?
   Yes, it was.
Didn't you have a second piece?
   Yes, I did.
Won't you be late?
   No, I won't.
Haven't you seen that movie already?
   Yes, I have.

MAKING REQUESTS

Would (Could) you lend me your notebook, please?
   Sure.
Could I borrow a pencil, please?
   I'm sorry. I don't have one.

DESCRIBING

It looks like a dog.
It sounds like a cat.
It feels like rubber.

The sweater is too big. It isn't small enough (to wear).
This sweater is so big I can't wear it.

COMPLIMENTING

What smells so good?
   A carrot cake.
It sounds terrific.
It looks great.

What delicious soup!
What a beautiful day!

COMPLAINING

It feels awful!
It tastes bad!

What an awful cake!
What sour oranges!
What awful weather!

TALKING ABOUT LIKES AND DISLIKES

I like ice cream because I like sweet things.
I hate potato chips because they're too salty.
I don't like lemonade because it's so sour.

What's the largest city in the world?

Listen as you read the conversation. Find out the meaning of the words you don't understand.

Keiko: Listen to this, Lynn. More people speak Chinese than any other language. The next most common language is English.

Lynn: I knew that. But English is an international language, and Chinese isn't. They speak English in the United States, Great Britain, Canada, Australia and New Zealand, and a lot of other places.

Keiko: Well, if you want to play Trivia, try this: What's the smallest country in the world?

Lynn: Vatican City.

Keiko: Right. OK, what's the largest city in the world?

Lynn: Mexico City or Tokyo.

Keiko: Mexico City. What's the biggest ocean?

Lynn: The Pacific.

Keiko: Right again. All right, what's the longest river in the world?

Lynn: That's a good question. Let's see. The Amazon?

Keiko: No. The Nile. What's the highest mountain?

Lynn: Mt. Everest in the Himalayas.

Keiko: Yeah. What's the largest desert?

Lynn: I don't know. The Gobi Desert in Asia?

Keiko: No. The Sahara Desert. OK. One more and I've had enough. I get tired of playing games like this. What's the biggest lake?

Lynn: Lake Superior is the biggest freshwater lake, isn't it? And the Caspian Sea is the biggest saltwater lake.

Keiko: Uh-huh. You got it.

Complete the chart with *the* when appropriate. Refer to the conversation on page 90 if you need help. Also fill in the information about your country.

Countries	Cities
_____ Russia	_____ Mexico City
_____ United States	_____ Tokyo
_____ China	_____ Shanghai
the Philippines	the Hague
_____ (*your* country)	_____ (a city in *your* country)

Rivers	Lakes
_____ Nile River	_____ Lake Superior
_____ Amazon River	_____ Lake Baykal
_____ Mississippi River	the Great Lakes
_____ (a river in *your* country)	_____ (a lake in *your* country)

Canals, Gulfs, Oceans, and Seas	Mountains
_____ Caspian Sea	_____ Mt. (Mount) Everest
_____ Pacific Ocean	_____ Mt. Fuji
_____ Caribbean Sea	_____ Himalayas
the Gulf of Mexico	_____ Rocky Mountains
the Panama Canal	_____ Andes
_____ (a body of water near *your* country)	_____ (a mountain or mountain range in *your* country)

Deserts	
_____ Sahara Desert	
_____ Gobi Desert	
_____ (a desert in *your* country)	

Ask questions using the words below. The answers are in the chart in exercise 1. Look at the example.

Vatican City

> small country
>
> **A:** What's **the smallest country** in the world?
> **B:** Vatican City.
> **A:** Right. (Yeah/Uh-huh/You got it.) OR No. It's _____ .

1. big country
2. large city
3. big ocean
4. long river
5. high mountains
6. large desert
7. big lake
8. Ask about things in your partner's country.

Listen and write the sentences. 🔲

1. Listen to this. _____
2. _____
3. _____
4. _____
5. _____
6. _____
7. _____
8. _____

Say the sentences in exercise 3 a different way.
Then listen and check your answers. 🔲

> **1.** Russia is larger than China.
> **China isn't as large as Russia.**

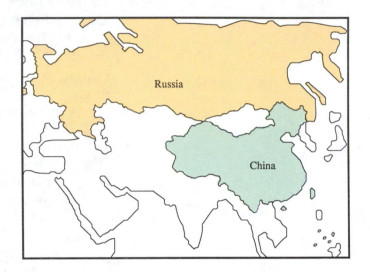

2. _____
3. _____
4. _____
5. _____
6. _____
7. _____
8. _____

Complete the conversations with the verbs in the list below. Then listen to them. 🔲

get tired (of)	get angry (with)	get upset (with)	get excited (by)
get sick (of)	get bored (with)	get embarrassed (by)	get confused (by)

A: I'm tired.
B: How come? (Why?)
A: This game is boring.
B: Yeah. I **get tired of** playing games like this, too.

A: I'm so angry!
B: What's the matter? (What's wrong?)
A: Look at this mess!
B: Yeah. I **get angry** when someone makes a mess, too.

(continued)

1. A: I'm sick of housework!
   B: _____
   A: It takes a lot of time.
   B: Yeah. I _____ doing housework, too.

2. A: I'm really upset.
   B: _____
   A: Frank didn't tell me the truth.
   B: Yeah. I _____ when someone lies to me, too.

3. A: I'm embarrassed!
   B: _____
   A: I didn't pass the English test.
   B: Yeah. I _____ when I fail a test, too.

4. A: I'm confused.
   B: _____
   A: I can't figure out the answer to this math problem.
   B: Yeah. I _____ math, too.

5. A: I'm so excited!
   B: _____
   A: I'm going to see my family next week.
   B: Yeah. I _____ when I see my family, too.

6. A: I'm bored!
   B: _____
   A: I don't like doing English homework.
   B: Yeah. I _____ homework, too.

EXERCISE 6

Talk to your classmates. Find someone who knows where . . .

1. the Philippines are.
   A: **Where are the Philippines?**
   B: **In the Pacific Ocean.**

	Name of Classmate
2. the Nile River is.	_____
3. the Eiffel Tower is.	_____
4. the smallest country is.	_____
5. the Gobi Desert is.	_____
6. the Hague is.	_____
7. the Amazon River is.	_____
8. the Great Lakes are.	_____
9. the Rocky Mountains are.	_____
10. Lake Superior is.	_____

Also find someone who . . .

11. gets upset when he or she doesn't know an answer.	_____
12. gets tired of playing games like this.	_____

Interesting statistics

Listen as you read the magazine article. Find out the meaning of the words you don't understand. 📼

JUST HOW BIG ARE THEY?

Russia is the largest country in the world. Vatican City is the smallest. Just how big are they? Russia is 6,593,000 square miles, and Vatican City is .17 square mile—that is, seventeen one-hundredths of a square mile.

The Nile is the longest river in the world. It flows through east Africa to the Mediterranean Sea. The biggest freshwater lake is Lake Superior between the United States and Canada. The deepest lake is Lake Baykal in Russia. The Sahara Desert in Africa is the largest desert. These are some of the natural wonders of the world.

Many other incredible wonders were built by people. For example, the tallest building is the Sears Tower in Chicago. It's big enough to hold 16,700 people. The longest wall is the Great Wall of China. How tall is the Sears Tower, and how long is the Great Wall? Look at the chart.

COUNTRIES (Area)		NATURAL WONDERS	
Russia	6,593,000 square miles	The Nile River	4,195 miles long
Vatican City	.17 square mile	The Caspian Sea	152,000 square miles
		Lake Superior	31,800 square miles
CITIES (Population)		Lake Baykal	6,365 feet deep
Mexico City	16,900,000	The Sahara Desert	3,500,000 square miles
Tokyo	12,000,000	Mt. Everest	29,000 feet high

The Nile River

The Great Wall

The Sears Tower

The Sahara Desert

NON-NATURAL WONDERS	
The Sears Tower	1,454 feet tall
The Great Wall of China	2,150 miles long
The Akashi-Kaikyo Bridge	11,680 feet long
The Sydney Harbour Bridge	160 feet wide

Match the descriptions with the answers. Scan the article on page 94 if you need help.

1. It's about 6,593,000 square miles.
2. It's .17 square mile.
3. It flows through east Africa to the Mediterranean Sea.
4. It's between the United States and Canada.
5. It's the deepest lake in the world.
6. It's the largest desert.
7. It can hold 16,700 people.
8. It's the widest bridge.

a. Lake Superior
b. the Sears Tower in Chicago
c. Russia
d. Lake Baykal in Russia
e. Vatican City
f. the Sahara Desert
g. the Nile
h. the Sydney Harbour Bridge

EXERCISE 2

First say the numbers. Then write them in words.

1. .17 **seventeen (one) hundredths**
2. 6.7 **six and seven-tenths**
3. 1,454 **one thousand four hundred (and) fifty-four**
4. 6,593,000 **six million five hundred (and) ninety-three thousand**

5. 2,150 _____
6. 6,365 _____
7. 11,680 _____
8. 31,800 _____
9. 152,000 _____
10. 16,900,000 _____

Now listen to the numbers. 🔲

EXERCISE 3

The chart on page 94 lists some of the smallest and biggest places in the world. For comparison, look up the information about your country. Then work with a partner. Ask questions about the chart and about your partner's country.

A: How *big* is *Russia*?
B: It's *6,593,000 square miles.*

A: How *long* is *the Nile River*?
B: It's *4,195 miles long.*

A: How *big* is (*your country*)?
B: It's ____ *square miles (kilometers).*

The size of your country ____ sq. mi/km
The population of your city ____
A natural wonder in your country ____
A non-natural wonder in your country ____

Listen for the correct information. Write numerals (10), not words (ten). 🔲

INTERESTING STATISTICS

1. About _____ people speak Mandarin Chinese.
2. Approximately _____ people around the world speak English.
3. Ten percent or more of the people in _____ different countries speak English.
4. There were about _____ telephones in the world in 1984.
5. In 1984, there were also approximately _____ cars in the world.
6. The Japanese National Railways carries _____ million people every day.
7. The best-selling record album of all time is *Thriller* by Michael Jackson. It has sold more than _____ million copies.
8. Every day the world's population increases by _____, or 149.9 people per minute.

After you check your answers, tell the class any other interesting statistics that you know.

Make sentences about things you didn't know until you began Unit 8. Look at and listen to the examples. 🔲

I didn't know (that) Vatican City is the smallest country in the world.
I had no idea (that) China is smaller than Russia.
I just learned (that) about 149.9 people are born per minute.

1. _____
2. _____
3. _____
4. _____

Report your answers to your partner like this:

A: **I had no idea (that)** *China was smaller than Russia.*
B: **I didn't either. (Oh, I knew that.)**

A: **I just learned (that)** *about 149.9 people are born per minute.*
B: **I did, too. (Oh, I knew that.)**

How big is it?

First try to guess the missing words. Then listen and check your guesses.

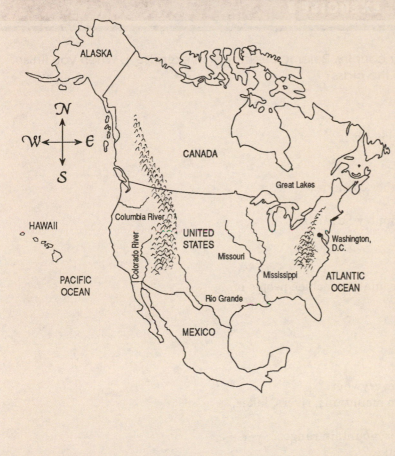

THE UNITED STATES

The United States is 1_____ large country. It is 3,623,420 square miles. The United 2_____ lies between the Pacific 3_____ Atlantic oceans. The country to the north is Canada. 4_____ country to the south 5_____ Mexico. The capital of the United States is Washington, D.C. The United States is divided into 50 6_____, and each state has 7_____ own capital city.

The population of the United States 8_____ almost 250,000,000. The population includes people of almost every race, religion, and nationality. Although 9_____ is the common language, 10_____ people speak Chinese, Spanish, Italian, and other languages.

The geography of the United States 11_____ extremely varied. There are mountains, 12_____, lakes, deserts, plains, and forests. The most 13_____ mountain ranges are 14_____ Appalachian Mountains in the east and the Rocky Mountains in the west. The most important rivers are the Mississippi 15_____ and the Missouri River in the middle of the country, and the Colorado and Columbia rivers 16_____ the west. The Rio Grande is the border 17_____ the United States and Mexico. The largest lakes are 18_____ Great Lakes between Canada 19_____ the United States.

Refer to the article on page 97 and choose the best answer.

1. *Lies* in paragraph 1 probably means
   a. is.
   b. isn't.
   c. doesn't tell the truth.

2. *Race* in paragraph 2 probably means
   a. run very fast.
   b. kind of people.
   c. experience.

3. *Varied* in paragraph 3 probably means
   a. the same in each part of the country.
   b. different in each part of the country.
   c. not very interesting.

4. *Border* in paragraph 3 probably means
   a. a place where one country ends and another country begins.
   b. a good place for Mexicans and Americans to swim.
   c. a place to the south.

Answer the questions and write about your country. Refer to the model in exercise 1. When you finish, read your composition to your group or to the class.

TITLE

Paragraph 1—The size of your country and where it is
1. Is your country large or small?
2. How big is it (area)?
3. Where is it? Is it on an ocean? Is it near other countries?
4. What's the capital?
5. How many states or divisions does your country have?

Paragraph 2—The people and the language
1. What's the population of your country?
2. Are all the people the same, or does the population include people of different races, religions, and nationalities?
3. What's the common language?
4. Do people speak any other languages?

Paragraph 3—The geography of your country
1. Is the geography varied, or is it the same everywhere?
2. If it's varied, how is it varied? Does it have mountains, rivers, lakes, deserts, plains, or forests?
3. What are the most important mountains or mountain ranges?
4. What are the most important rivers and lakes?

Work with a group or with the class and play Trivia. Make up your own questions or use the model questions.

1. What's the largest country in the world?
2. What's the highest mountain in the world?
3. What's the largest desert?
4. Ask your own questions.

5. How many people are born per minute?
6. How high is Mt. Everest?
7. How long is the Nile?
8. Ask your own questions.

9. Name two countries that are islands.
10. Name the longest river in Brazil.
11. Name four oceans.
12. Ask your own questions.

GRAMMAR SUMMARY

REVIEW: THE SUPERLATIVE OF ADJECTIVES

What's **the longest** river in the world?
The Nile is **the longest** river.

REVIEW: THE COMPARATIVE OF ADJECTIVES

Russia is **larger than** China.
China isn't **as large as** Russia.

INFORMATION (WH-) QUESTIONS: *HOW* **+ ADJECTIVE**

How big is Russia?
How long is the Nile River?

GET **+ ADJECTIVE**

I **get angry** when someone makes a mess.
I **get tired** of playing games like this.

NUMBERS

seventeen one-hundredths/point seventeen (**.17**)
six and seven-tenths/six point seven (**6.7**)
one thousand four hundred (and) fifty-four (**1,454**)
six million five hundred (and) ninety-three thousand (**6,593,000**)

THE **WITH GEOGRAPHICAL NAMES AND PLACES**

Countries
China

Exceptions:
   United—**the United** States
   plural word—**the** Philippines

Cities
Tokyo

Exception: **the** Hague

Rivers
the Amazon River

Deserts
the Sahara Desert

Lakes
Lake Superior

Exception:
   plural word—**the** Great Lakes

Canals, Gulfs, Oceans, and Seas
the Caspian Sea
the Pacific Ocean
the Gulf of Mexico
the Panama Canal

Mountains and Mountain Ranges
Mt. Fuji
the Andes

Buildings and Monuments
the Sears Tower
the Great Wall of China
the Akashi-Kaikyo Bridge

VOCABULARY

approximately
common
deep
division
geographically
geography
incredible
international
Mandarin Chinese
national
natural
non-natural
population
race
railways
religion
separate
statistic
thriller
through
trivia
varied
wonder

GEOGRAPHY

area
border
canal
capital
desert
forest
freshwater
gulf
harbour (harbor)
island
mountain range
Mt. (Mount)
ocean
plain
saltwater
sea
square kilometer (km)
square mile
state

DIRECTIONS

east
north
south
west

VERBS

fail
flow
include
lie (not tell the truth)
lie [lay/lain] (be in a place)
pass (a test)
get [got/gotten] angry (with)
get bored (with)
get confused (by)
get embarrassed (by)
get excited (by)
get sick (of)
get tired (of)
get upset (with)

COMMUNICATION SUMMARY

TALKING ABOUT GEOGRAPHY

What's the smallest country in the world?
    Vatican City.
How big is Russia?
    It's 6,593,000 square miles.
How long is the Nile River?
    It's 4,195 miles long.

COMPARING PLACES

Russia is larger than China.
China isn't as large as Russia.

CONFIRMING

Right.
Uh-huh.
You got it.

ASKING FOR EXPLANATIONS

How come?
Why?
What's the matter?
What's wrong?

EXPRESSING POSITIVE AND NEGATIVE FEELINGS

I'm tired!
    I get tired of playing games like this, too.
I'm so excited!
    I get excited when I see my family, too.

TALKING ABOUT WHAT YOU'VE LEARNED

I didn't know (that) Vatican City is the smallest country in the world.
    I didn't either.
I had no idea (that) China was smaller than Russia.
    Oh, I knew that.
I just learned (that) about 149.9 people are born per minute.
    I did, too.

GIVING STATISTICS

Approximately 400,000,000 people around the world speak English.
About 149.9 people are born per minute.

LESSON
1

It seems like everything is imported.

Listen as you read the conversation. Find out the meaning of the words you don't understand.

Victor: What a nice camera!

Roberto: Thanks. It's Japanese.

Victor: Isn't this country incredible? It seems like everything is imported.

Roberto: Yeah. TVs, stereos, and cameras are often made in Japan. You can get running shoes from Korea. Clothes are made in Hong Kong and Taiwan. Watches are imported from France and Switzerland.

Victor: Even fruit and vegetables are imported from Mexico and Chile during the winter.

Roberto: Yes. And a lot of cars are imported, too. I think Americans are fascinated by foreign products.

Victor: Well, sometimes they're designed better. And sometimes they're a lot cheaper, too.

Roberto: Say, have you got the time? I want to take some pictures before class tonight.

Victor: It's 3:00.

Roberto: Oh, I'd better go. It's getting late.

Victor: Yeah. I'd better go, too. I haven't done my homework yet.

Refer to the conversation on page 102 again. Then answer *That's right, That's wrong,* or *It doesn't say.* Correct the statements that are wrong.

1. Americans often buy foreign cameras, TVs, stereos, and cars.
2. Koreans sometimes buy American running shoes.
3. American clothes sometimes come from Hong Kong and Taiwan.
4. Americans never import watches from Europe.
5. Americans import onions and potatoes from Mexico.
6. Other countries often make cheaper cars, stereos, and clothes than the United States.
7. Roberto thinks he should go so he'll have enough time to take some pictures before class.
8. Victor thinks he should go so he can take a shower before class.

What kinds of products are grown or made in the United States? Make sentences.

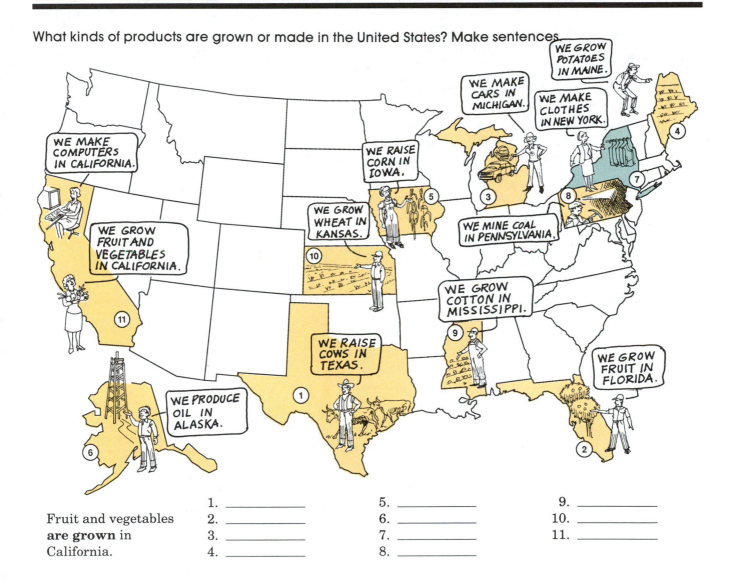

Fruit and vegetables **are grown** in California.

1. _____
2. _____
3. _____
4. _____
5. _____
6. _____
7. _____
8. _____
9. _____
10. _____
11. _____

What kinds of things are grown or made in *your* country? Tell your group or the class.

Complete the sentences with *for, before, during,* and *after.* Refer to Gina's calendar.

> Gina has a meeting with Mrs. White **before** lunch.

1. Gina is going to ask Mr. Lopez for a raise _____ lunch.
2. She's going to meet Frank _____ lunch.
3. _____ lunch, she's going to talk to Frank about paying the rent.
4. She has to buy pens for the office _____ lunch.

5. She has to do her homework _____ class.
6. She's going to have a sandwich _____ class.
7. She's going to ask about the new grammar _____ class.
8. She's going to meet Frank _____ class.

After you check your answers, answer these questions about yourself.

9. What do you do before breakfast?
10. What do you eat for breakfast?
11. What do you do during breakfast?
12. What do you do after breakfast?

23 Monday March 1993   **23**

8:00
9:00 write to National Exports
10:00 meeting with Mrs. White
11:00 ask Mr. Lopez for a raise
12:00 lunch with Frank, talk about paying rent
1:00 buy pens
2:00
3:00
4:00
5:00 do homework and have a sandwich

Evening
7:30 English class
  ask Mrs. Brennan
  about new grammar
8:30 meet Frank

Monday, March 23, 1993

Look at the signs and give your partner some strong advice as in the examples. Then listen to the exchanges.

be quiet
A: *Talking* **isn't allowed here. You'd better** *be quiet.*
B: **Oh, I didn't see the sign.**

not play here
A: *Ball playing* **isn't allowed here. You'd better** *not play here.*
B: **Oh, I didn't see the sign.**

1. put out your cigarette
A: _____
B: _____

2. not park here
A: _____
B: _____

3. not take any food into the museum
A: _____
B: _____

4. turn it off
A: _____
B: _____

5. pick up those papers
A: _____
B: _____

6. not go in the water
A: _____
B: _____

Pretend you have something to do (a date, a meeting, a class, etc.). Ask the time and then give yourself some advice. Listen to the example.

A: *Victor,* **have you got the time?**
B: **Yeah, it's** *3:00.*
A: **I'd better** *go. I haven't done my homework yet.*
        OR
I have a date at 3:30. **I'd better not** *be late.*

Gina and Frank are having lunch. Listen and complete their conversation.

Gina: Frank, we've got a problem. We don't have enough money to pay the rent this month.
Frank: I know. I guess I'd better ask Mom and Dad for a loan.
Gina: And ¹_____ .
Frank: ²_____ ?
Gina: I don't know. But maybe I'd better not take another English course for a while.
Frank: Gina, you can't stop studying English. It's important. ³_____ . You can't get ahead without English.
Gina: I know.
Frank: ⁴_____ . I can work at the office during the day and then do something else at night. In fact, ⁵_____ .

Where was this taken?

Listen as you read the conversation. Find out the meaning of the words you don't understand.

Olga: You know, we've never seen the pictures you took of New York.
Roberto: No? Didn't I show them to you after I got back?
Victor: No.
Roberto: Well, I have them with me . . . . This is the Empire State Building. It's probably the most famous building in New York. It was built in less than two years. It was begun in 1929 and finished in 1931.
Susan: Isn't that incredible?
Roberto: This is the United Nations.
Olga: It was built sometime after World War I ended, wasn't it?
Victor: After World War II.
Olga: I mean World War II. Where was this taken?
Roberto: From the top of the World Trade Center. Did you know the Statue of Liberty was designed by a Frenchman?
Victor: Uh-huh. Bartholdi. It was given to the United States by France on the 100th birthday of U.S. independence.
Susan: You know a lot about history.
Victor: History was my favorite subject in school—after music, that is!

Refer to the conversation on page 106 again and correct these statements.

1. Roberto hasn't been to New York.
2. The Empire State Building isn't very famous.
3. The Empire State Building was built in less than a year.
4. The UN was built after World War I.
5. The Statue of Liberty was given to the United States by England.

EXERCISE 2

Listen to each sentence. Write the city or country and the date. 🔲

1. The Statue of Liberty was given to _____ in _____ .
2. The Eiffel Tower was built in _____ in _____ .
3. The Golden Gate Bridge was built in _____ in _____ .
4. The Empire State Building was built in _____ in _____ .
5. The Pyramids were built in _____ around _____ B.C.
6. The Sears Tower was built in _____ in _____ .
7. The temples at Angkor Wat were built in _____ in the _____ century.
8. Corcovado was built in _____ in _____ .
9. The Sydney Opera House was built in _____ in _____ .
10. The Colosseum was built in _____ in _____ A.D.

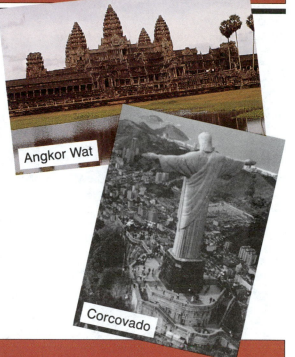

Angkor Wat

Corcovado

EXERCISE 3

Combine the sentences with *when, before,* or *after.* Look at the examples.

The UN was built in 1950. World War II ended in 1946.
The UN was built **after** World War II ended.
The Sears Tower was the tallest building in the world. It was completed in 1974.
When it was completed in 1974, the Sears Tower was the tallest building in the world.

1. The Statue of Liberty was built in France. Then it was sent to the United States.
2. The World Trade Center Towers were the tallest buildings in the world. They were completed in 1972.
3. The Colosseum was built in Rome. The Parthenon was built in Athens about 500 years earlier.
4. The Eiffel Tower was finished. Then the 1889 World's Fair opened in France.

Now give complete answers to these questions about yourself.

5. Did you ever think about studying English when you were little?
6. Did you start studying English before or after you finished elementary school?
7. When you had to speak English for the first time, were you excited or embarrassed?

When were the things designed, built, painted, or written? Ask questions. Listen to the example. 📼

A: **When was** *Another Country written*?
B: **It was** *written in 1982*.
A: *1962*.
B: **I mean** *1962*.
A: **Where was it** *written*?
B: **(It was** *written)* **in** *France*.
A: **Who was it** *written* **by?**
B: **It was** *written* **by** *James Baldwin*.

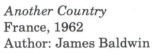

Another Country
France, 1962
Author: James Baldwin

1. The Statue of Liberty
   France, 1885
   Sculptor: Frederic Auguste
   Bartholdi

Vincent van Gogh
Oleanders

2. *Oleanders*
   France, 1888
   Painter: Vincent van Gogh

3. *Emma*
   England, 1816
   Author: Jane Austen

4. The Guggenheim Museum
   New York City, 1959
   Architect: Frank Lloyd Wright

5. Brasilia
   Brazil, 1960
   Architect: Oscar Niemeyer

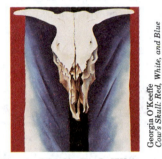

Georgia O'Keeffe
Cow's Skull: Red, White, and Blue

6. *Cow's Skull: Red, White and Blue*
   New York, 1931
   Painter: Georgia O'Keeffe

Bring to class a picture of your favorite building, painting, or sculpture or a copy of your favorite book. Work with a group. Your classmates will ask you questions about your picture or book.

What's this called?
Where was it done?
When was it done?
Who was it done by?

Henry Moore
Family Group (1945-49)
Collection, The Museum of
Modern Art, New York, A.
Conger Goodyear Fund

Compliment a classmate. Follow the examples.

A: **What a** *nice watch*!
B: **Thanks. It's** *Japanese*. OR
   It was made in *Japan*. OR
   It's new. OR
   It was a gift from _____ .

A: **What** *nice earrings*!
B: **Thanks. They** _____ .

LESSON 3

A tour

Listen to the tour guide and write the dates you hear. 📼

1. The Washington Monument, completed in _____
2. The Jefferson Memorial, dedicated in _____
3. The White House, rebuilt in _____
4. The National Gallery of Art, opened in _____
5. The Lincoln Memorial, built in _____

Now scan this page from a guide to Washington, D.C., to check the dates you wrote and to find the missing dates.

Washington, D.C. (District of Columbia) is the capital of the United States. It became the capital on December 1, 1880. It was named for George Washington, the first president, and Christopher Columbus (America was discovered by Columbus in 1492).

Spring is the best season in Washington, and it is the most popular with tourists. In the spring you can see the flowers on hundreds of cherry trees. The trees were given to the United States in 1912. They were a gift of friendship from Japan.

Washington has something for everyone—historic monuments, interesting museums, beautiful parks, and excellent hotels and restaurants. Some of the most important and most interesting sights are:

The Jefferson Memorial. This monument is dedicated to the third president, Thomas Jefferson. It was designed by John Russel, and it was dedicated in 1943. Inside there is a statue of Jefferson by sculptor Rudolf Evans.

The Lincoln Memorial. This beautiful monument is dedicated to Abraham Lincoln, the sixteenth president of the United States. It is made of marble, and it was built in 1922. In the great hall there is a huge statue of Lincoln by Daniel Chester French.

Lincoln Memorial

Washington Monument

National Gallery of Art

The National Gallery of Art. The National Gallery contains one of the world's best collections of European and American painting and sculpture. The newest building, the East Building, is made of pink marble and glass. It was designed by I. M. Pei, and it was opened in 1978.

The Washington Monument. The Washington Monument was completed in 1884. It is dedicated to our first president, George Washington, and it is 555 feet high. You can take an elevator to the top or you can climb the 898 steps!

The White House. The White House is the official home of the president. It was designed by James Hoban. The first building was burned by the British in the War of 1812, but it was rebuilt in 1818. It was also first painted white at that time.

Jefferson Memorial

White House

Read the page from the guide to Washington, D.C., on page 109. Then answer these questions.

1. Who was Washington, D.C., named for?
2. Where did the cherry trees come from?
3. How tall is the Washington Monument?
4. When was the White House first painted white?

5. Who is the Jefferson Memorial dedicated to?
6. Who designed it?
7. What is the Lincoln Memorial made of?
8. Who designed the statue of Lincoln?

After you check your answers, ask your own questions about the National Gallery of Art.

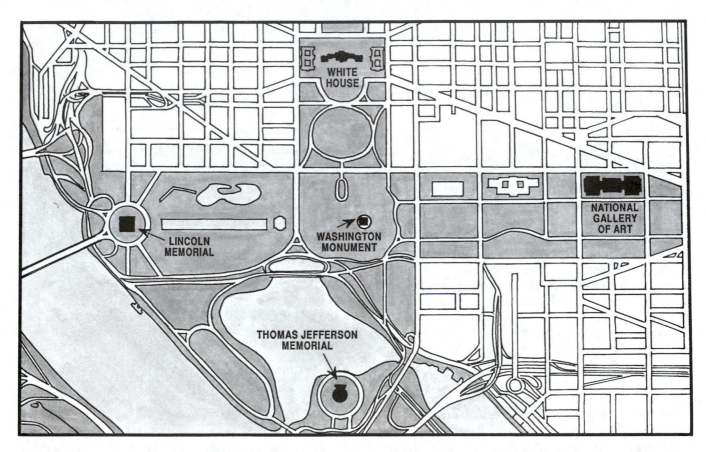

Work with a group. Decide which place in the guide you will visit. Use the ideas in the list and your own ideas. Choose only *one* place.

I'd really like to go to/visit _____ .
That might be interesting, but I think the _____ sounds exciting.
What about the _____ ? It's _____ .
Yeah, that sounds good.
I agree. Let's go there.
Fine with me.

Answer the questions and write about the capital or an important city in your country. Pretend you are writing this information for tourists. Refer to the guide in exercise 1 for help.

Paragraph 1—Background
1. What is the name of the city?
2. When did this city become the capital, or when was it built?
3. Who was the city named for, or what does the name mean in English?

Paragraph 2—The best time to go
1. What is the best season or time of year to visit the city?
2. Why is this time best or special?

Paragraph 3—What does the city offer?
1. What does the city have for tourists? Sights? Hotels? Restaurants? Nightlife?
2. Give some information about one or two important or interesting sights.

EXERCISE 5

Talk to your classmates. Find out . . .

1. if a classmate owns something from another country.
2. where a classmate's watch was made.
3. what is imported by a classmate's country.
4. where it is imported from.
5. what is exported by a classmate's country.
6. who painted the Mona Lisa.
7. where ice cream was first made.
8. Ask your own question.

GRAMMAR SUMMARY

REVIEW: GERUNDS

Smoking isn't allowed here.

REVIEW: *WHAT* (A/AN)

What a nice watch!
What nice earrings!

PASSIVE VOICE: PRESENT

What	's	this	**called?**	

| **It** | **'s** | | **called** | Corcovado. |
| Vegetables | **are** | | **imported** | from Chile. |

PASSIVE VOICE: PAST

When	**was**	it	**built?**	

| It | **was** | | **built** | in 1885. |
| The buildings | **were** | | **completed** | in 1972. |

HAD BETTER

You	**'d better**	**(not)**	**go.**

***BEFORE, DURING*, AND *AFTER* + NOUN**

She's going to ask about the grammar	**before** **during** **after**	class.

***BEFORE, AFTER*, AND *WHEN* + CLAUSE**

The Parthenon was built about 500 years	**before**	the Colosseum was built.
The Empire State Building was finished two years	**after**	it was begun.
The Sears Tower was the tallest building	**when**	it was completed in 1974.

Before it was sent to the United States,	the Statue of Liberty was designed in France.
After World War II ended,	the UN was built.
When it was completed in 1974,	the Sears Tower was the tallest building.

VOCABULARY

A.D.
author
B.C.
center
coal
collection
cotton
drama
entertainment
friendship
historic
loan
marble
monument
nightlife
official
painter
product
raise
sculptor
sculpture
skull
wheat

the top of
World War II

VERBS

allow
complete
contain
dedicate
export
get [got/gotten] ahead
grow [grew/grown]
import
mine
produce
put out (a fire)
raise
rebuild [rebuilt/rebuilt]
seem

COMMUNICATION SUMMARY

FINDING OUT THE TIME

Have you got the time?
    Yeah. It's 3:00.

STATING RULES

Smoking isn't allowed here.

ASKING FOR PERSONAL INFORMATION

What do you do before breakfast?
    I jog.
What do you do during breakfast?
    I read the newspaper.
What do you do after breakfast?
    I go to work.

TALKING ABOUT FAMOUS PLACES AND THINGS

What's this called?
    It's called *Oleanders*.
When was it painted?
    It was painted in 1888.
Who was it painted by?
    It was painted by Vincent van Gogh.

TALKING ABOUT PRODUCTS

Cotton is grown in Mississippi.
Fruit and vegetables are imported from Mexico and Chile.

GIVING STRONG ADVICE

You'd better put out your cigarette.
You'd better not play here.

GIVING ONESELF ADVICE

I'd better go.
I'd better not be late.

CORRECTING SOMEONE AND ONESELF

It was built in 1985.
    1885.
I mean 1885.

COMPLIMENTING

What a nice watch!
What nice earrings!

TALKING ABOUT THE PAST

The Parthenon was built about 500 years before the Colosseum was built.
The Empire State Building was finished two years after it was begun.
The Eiffel Tower was finished when the 1889 World's Fair opened in France.
I was embarrassed when I tried to speak English the first time.

If I were you, I'd fly.

Listen as you read the conversation. Find out the meaning of the words you don't understand.

Lynn: What are you going to do during class break?
Tony: I hope to go camping with Pierre. We want to go to the Grand Canyon. How about you?
Lynn: I plan to buy a car and drive to Los Angeles.
Tony: What's in Los Angeles?
Lynn: I have a friend there.
Tony: L.A. is a long way. If I were you, I'd fly. You can fly safely and cheaply these days. And you can always rent a car in L.A.
Lynn: No. I want to drive. Say, would you come with me if I paid for the gas and everything? You could go camping some other time.
Tony: No. I really want to see the Grand Canyon, and I've already bought a new backpack. Besides, what would I tell Pierre if I went with you?
Lynn: What do you mean?
Tony: Well, going camping was his idea, and he lent me the money for the backpack.

114

Match the two parts of each sentence.

1. Tony hopes to	a. buy a car.
2. Tony wants to	b. visit a friend in Los Angeles.
3. Lynn plans to	c. go camping with Pierre.
4. Lynn doesn't want to	d. fly to Los Angeles.
5. She wants to	e. see the Grand Canyon.
6. She plans to	f. drive.

EXERCISE 2

First complete the chart. Then complete the conversations as in the example. After you finish, listen to the conversations. 🔲

A: Flying is **quick** and **safe**.
B: I agree. You can fly **quickly** and **safely** these days.

Adjective	Adverb
cheap	cheaply
quick	_____
safe	_____
efficient	_____
smooth	_____
bad	_____
economical	economically
careful	_____
good	well
hard	hard
fast	fast

1. A: Driving to L.A. isn't *fast*, but it's _____ .
   B: That's true. Maybe you can't drive _____ , but you can drive *cheaply*.

2. A: My new car is very _____ . It has an *efficient* engine.
   B: I'm glad it runs *economically* and _____ .

3. A: My car isn't a *good* car for highways, but the ride is pretty _____ at low speeds.
   B: My car is the same. It doesn't drive _____ on highways, but it drives *smoothly* around town.

4. A: My car is *hard* to drive. In fact, I have to be very _____ in traffic.
   B: Well, you shouldn't have to work so _____ . It's a new car. But it's always a good idea to drive *carefully* in traffic.

5. Describe your or your family's car.

6. What kind of driver are you, and how do you drive?

7. How do you think most people drive?

Look at the example and answer the questions. Then work with a group and find out about your classmates.

> **A:** **How economically** does your car run?
> **B:** It doesn't run economically at all. It uses a lot of gas and oil.

1. How fast do you usually drive?
2. How cheaply can you eat every day?
3. How badly do you want to learn English?
4. How hard do you study?
5. How carefully do you do your homework?
6. How well do you understand this lesson?

Ask for and give advice. Complete the conversations with *should* and *would ('d)* or *would not (wouldn't)*. Then listen to them.

> **A:** **Should** I fly or drive?
> **B:** Well, if I were you, I'd fly. I wouldn't drive. Besides, you can fly quickly and cheaply.

1. A: _____ I buy a new car or fix my old one?
   B: _____ . _____ . Besides, your old one is in pretty good condition.

2. A: _____ I study or go to the movies?
   B: _____ . _____ . Besides, you want to pass the test, don't you?

3. A: _____ I rent or buy?
   B: _____ . _____ . Besides, you don't have a lot of money right now.

4. A: _____ I take bookkeeping or learn how to use a computer?
   B: _____ . _____ . Besides, there are a lot of jobs for people with computer experience.

5. A: _____ I make a cake or buy a pie?
   B: _____ . _____ . Besides, it's easier to buy a pie than to make a cake.

Tony is reading a letter from his sister. First try to guess the missing words. Then listen and check your guesses. 📼

Dear Tony,

Mom told me you are planning to go to the Grand Canyon with your friend Pierre. The Grand Canyon is an incredible place. It's really beautiful. I went there when I was in the U.S. However, if I **1**_____ you, I **2**_____ go in the summer. I **3**_____ go in the winter. The Grand Canyon is very cold in the winter and I don't think you **4**_____ enjoy yourself if you **5**_____ then. Also, if it **6**_____, you **7**_____ be able to walk around and see things very well.

If I **8**_____ you, I **9**_____ go someplace warm. In fact, I **10**_____ think about going to California. Maybe one of the other students **11**_____ drive if you **12**_____ to pay for the gas. Maybe Pierre **13**_____ go too if you **14**_____ him. I mean, if you **15**_____ him you **16**_____ go to the Grand Canyon next summer, he **17**_____ probably go to California with you during your class break. **18**_____ you like all of that sunny weather and the beaches? I know I would!

Let me know what you decide.

Love,
Paula

Answer these questions about the first paragraph of Paula's letter.

1. Would Paula go to the Grand Canyon if she were Tony?
2. Would Tony enjoy himself if he went to the Grand Canyon in winter?
3. Would he be able to walk around easily and see things well if it snowed?

Now ask your own questions about the second paragraph of the letter.

Talk to your classmates. Find out what a classmate would do if he or she . . .

1. didn't understand the grammar in this unit.
2. had a headache.
3. saw a robber in a bank.
4. spilled coffee on a classmate's desk.
5. were tired.

Find out how a classmate would feel if . . .

6. a friend lied to him or her.
7. he or she lent a friend some money and the friend didn't pay it back.
8. he or she won $25,000.
9. he or she failed the next English test.

How well do they handle?

Listen as you read the conversation. Find out the meaning of the words you don't understand.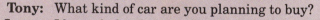

Tony: What kind of car are you planning to buy?
Lynn: I haven't decided yet. Something economical.
Tony: I think that Comets are pretty economical. They're small, and I know they don't use much gas.
Lynn: Yes, but how well do they handle on the highway? I've heard that they handle badly at high speeds.
Tony: I don't know. I've never driven one.
Lynn: Actually, I'm thinking about a Galaxy. I believe they drive better than Comets, especially in bad weather.
Tony: Really? *Consumer Magazine* says the Comet is the most efficient car on the market. It has a new kind of engine and, like I said, it doesn't use a lot of gas.
Lynn: Well, it might run the most efficiently and it might not use much gas, but I don't think it drives very smoothly. My sister has one, and she hates it. She says it steers hard and it doesn't brake well.
Tony: Well, I hope you make the right decision.
Lynn: So do I.
Tony: And I really feel that you should check *Consumer Magazine*.

Refer to the conversation on page 118. Answer True (T) or False (F) and correct the false statements.

1. Lynn is probably going to buy a Comet.
2. Tony thinks Comets are economical and efficient.
3. Lynn isn't sure that Comets run efficiently.
4. Galaxies don't run well in bad weather.
5. *Consumer Magazine* says the Comet is more efficient than the Galaxy.
6. If Tony were Lynn, he'd buy a Galaxy.

	T	F

EXERCISE 2

Are the sentences in the article from *Consumer Magazine* drawing conclusions *(must)*, giving advice *(should/ought to)*, talking about possibility *(might/may)*, or talking about ability *(can)*? Complete the article with the appropriate words. Then listen and check your answers. 📼

THE COMET IS BEST FOR DESIGN, ECONOMY, AND PERFORMANCE

Does your old car make a lot of noise? Does it use a lot of gas? Does it drive badly on the highway? Then you **must** need a new car.

Before you buy a new car, however, you really **1**_____ take a look at the new Comet. You **2**_____ be surprised by this year's model. It has a new engine, and it doesn't use much gasoline. It is the most efficient car on the market.

Besides the new engine, there are several new colors of paint and special matching interiors. You **3**_____ choose evening gray, sunset red, midnight blue, or cloud white. You **4**_____ select matching leather or plastic seats. And every car today **5**_____ have a stereo cassette player, so every new Comet has one at no extra cost.

You **6**_____ not buy a car if it doesn't drive smoothly, and you **7**_____ not be happy if your new car uses too much gas. So we suggest that you drive the Comet and test it for yourself. You **8**_____ like the way it handles. It steers easily and brakes well. And it is economical on gas.

If you don't choose a Comet, you **9**_____ not be worried about economy and performance. And you **10**_____ not need to think about price.

Read the ads and answer the questions.

WASH-O-MATIC	QUICKWASH	SureSpeed
holds 8 lb. uses $\frac{1}{2}$ cup soap takes 20 minutes	holds 8 lb. uses $\frac{3}{4}$ cup soap takes 20 minutes	holds 10 lb. uses $\frac{1}{2}$ cup soap takes 18 minutes
uses less water than the Quickwash	washes better than all other machines	uses less water than the Quickwash and the Wash-O-Matic
energy efficiency rating: 9 sale price: **$450**	energy efficiency rating: 8.5 sale price: **$459**	energy efficiency rating: 10 sale price: **$449**

1. According to the ads, which machine washes faster, the Quickwash or the SureSpeed?
2. Which machine washes more slowly, the Quickwash or the SureSpeed?
3. Which machine washes better, the Quickwash or the SureSpeed?
4. Which company sells its washing machines more cheaply, Quickwash or SureSpeed?
5. Which washing machine runs more economically, the Wash-O-Matic or the Quickwash? Why is it more economical?
6. Which machine works more efficiently, the Quickwash or the SureSpeed? Why is it more efficient?

Refer to the ads in exercise 3 and ask and answer questions. Listen to the example.

> the most economical/economically
>
> A: **Which washing machine runs** *the most economically*?
>
> B: *The SureSpeed* **runs** *the most economically* **of all.**
>
> A: **How do you know it's** *the most economical*?
>
> B: **Because, according to the ad,** *it takes only 18 minutes and it uses less water than the other machines.*

1. the most efficient/efficiently
2. the fastest
3. the most slowly/the slowest
4. the best

Work with a group. Pretend you need a new washing machine for the laundry room in your apartment building. If you had to buy a new machine, which one would you buy? You can use the information in the list.

The ad says the . . . runs . . .
The . . . (holds/is/runs/works) . . .
I think we should buy a . . . because . . .
If I had to buy a washing machine, I'd . . . because . . .

LESSON 3 School break

EXERCISE 1

Answer these questions before you look at the table in exercise 2.

1. What different kinds of vehicles can you think of?
2. What is the most common form of transportation in your country?
3. What is the most economical way to travel?

EXERCISE 2

Before you look at the table, try to guess the answers to these questions.

1. Are there more cars, motorcycles, buses, or trucks on the road in the United States?
2. Do cars, motorcycles, buses, or trucks use more gas?
3. Do the engines in cars, motorcycles, buses, or trucks run the most efficiently?
4. Are cars, motorcycles, buses, or trucks the most expensive to run?

ANNUAL U.S. MOTOR VEHICLE STATISTICS				
Type of Vehicle	Number of Vehicle	Miles Traveled per Vehicle	Gallons of Gas per Vehicle	Miles per Gallon
Cars	132,108,164	9,827	549	17.90
Motorcyles	5,444,404	2,204	44	50.00
Buses	593,527	11,678	2,072	5.64
Trucks	38,989,042	11,737	1,215	9.66

Source: Department of Transportation, Federal Highway Administration, as published in the *1988 Information Please Almanac.*

Now scan the table for the answers to the questions above. Did you guess correctly? Can you answer the question below?

5. If they only had to pay for gas, which group could travel more economically, five passengers in a car or twenty passengers in a bus?

UNIT 10   **121**

Read the statistics in this table. Then work with a group and ask and answer questions as in the example.

a 16-year-old/a 60-year-old/usually drive fast

A: *Does a 16-year-old or a 60-year-old usually drive faster?*

B: I've read (*that*) *a 16-year-old drives faster.*
OR
I've heard (*that*) *a 16-year-old drives faster.* OR
I think (*that*) *a 16-year-old drives faster.*

C: So have I. (So do I.) OR
Really? I've read/I think . . .

1. young people/older people/usually drive carefully
2. men/women/usually drive fast
3. men/women/usually drive dangerously
4. a young person/an older person/usually drive slowly
5. Ask questions about different groups of people in your country.

MOTOR VEHICLE DEATHS FROM ACCIDENTS IN 1984
(Usual causes: speeding or carelessness)

Age and Sex	Total Deaths
15 to 24 years	14,738
25 to 44 years	15,036
45 to 64 years	6,954
65 to 74 years	3,020
Men	32,949
Women	13,314

Source: National Safety Control, 1984 Statistics, as published in the *1988 World Almanac.*

Mr. Stein is talking to his class. What are his students going to do during class break? Listen and find out.

Student	Work	Take A Trip	Visit His or Her Family	Undecided
1. John				
2. Anna				
3. Maria				
4. Peter				
5. Alex				
6. Sue				
7. Pablo				
8. Laura				

Find out what your partner is going to do during class break or when this course ends. Use some of the verbs in the list. Follow the examples.

plan	hope
like	enjoy
want	would like
love	look forward to

A: **What are you going to do** *during the class break*?
B: **I** *hope to go camping.*
(**I'm not planning to do anything.**)
A: **Oh, really?**
B: **Yeah.** *I love being outdoors.*
(**I'm a little broke right now.**)

Capitalize and punctuate this postcard. Use 13 capital letters, and add 13 punctuation marks.

july 15 1994

marjorie
i plan to go to the grand canyon during the spring break it's a beautiful place and i'm looking forward to going there i know you haven t been there before so would you like to go with me it wouldn t be an expensive trip if we drove would you go if i paid for the gas and everything let me know as soon as possible
maria

Marjorie Chin
1233 Van Ness Street
San Francisco CA 94109

Write a postcard to a friend. Answer these questions in your postcard.

1. Where do you plan to go (during your school break/after your class ends/on vacation)?
2. What do you want to do there?
3. Has your friend been to this place?
4. Ask your friend to go with you.
5. Would the trip be expensive? Why?
6. Say what you would do so your friend could accept your invitation.
7. Do you want your friend to let you know his or her decision? When?

Try to convince your partner to go somewhere with you. Use the ideas in the list. Listen to the example.

A: **Would you** *go to Los Angeles* **with me if I** *paid for the gas and everything*?
B: **I guess so.** OR
No, I really don't *want to go there.*

do all the driving	pay for your hotel
pay for your ticket	not stay too long
lend you the money	help you . . .
buy your meals	your own ideas

REVIEW: *MIGHT (MAY), SHOULD (OUGHT TO), MUST, AND CAN*

You **might** be surprised by this year's model.
You **can** choose evening gray or sunset red.
You **should** take a look at the new Comet.
You **must** need a new car.

REVIEW: VERB + INFINITIVE OR GERUND

I **hope to go** camping.
I **love being** outdoors.

REVIEW: ADJECTIVES AND ADVERBS

Flying is **quick** and **safe**.
You can fly **quickly** and **safely**.

INFORMATION (WH-) QUESTIONS: *HOW* + ADVERB

How fast do you usually drive?
How badly do you want to learn English?

THE COMPARATIVE AND SUPERLATIVE OF ADVERBS

Do young people or older people drive	**more carefully?**	
I've read that older people drive	**more carefully than**	young people.
Which machine washes	**better,**	the Quickwash or the SureSpeed?
The Quickwash washes	**better than**	the SureSpeed.

Do cars, motorcycles, buses, or trucks run	**the most economically?**	
Motorcycles run	**the most economically.**	
Which washing machine washes	**the best?**	
The Quickwash washes	**the best**	of all.

THE CONDITIONAL WITH *IF . . . WOULD* (HYPOTHETICAL SITUATIONS)

Information (Wh-) Questions

What	**would**	you	**do**	**if**	you	**were**	tired?
		she			she	**had**	a headache?
		they			they	**didn't have**	any aspirin?

Statements

I	**'d (would) rest.**	
She	**'d take**	an aspirin.
They	**wouldn't do**	anything.

If	I	**were**	you,	I	**'d rest.**

Yes/No Questions

Would	you	**go**	to Los Angeles with me	**if**	I	**paid**	for everything?

Short Answers

Yes, I **would.**/No, I **wouldn't.**

VOCABULARY

annual
backpack
carelessness
cause
cheaply
cost
dangerously
death
economically
economy
efficiency
efficient
efficiently
energy
engine
final
interior
matching
model
performance
quick
rating
safely
sex
smooth
smoothly
soap
speed
speeding
sunset
traffic
type
undecided
usual

Besides, . . .

VERBS

be broke
brake
go camping
handle
pay [paid/paid] back
run [ran/run] (a
   machine/engine)
snow
steer
take [took/taken] a look at

COMMUNICATION SUMMARY

ASKING FOR AND GIVING ADVICE

Should I fly or drive?
   Well, if I were you, I'd drive.

GIVING ADDITIONAL INFORMATION

Besides, you can fly safely and cheaply.

TALKING ABOUT HOW PEOPLE DO THINGS

How fast do most people drive?
   They drive pretty fast.
Do young people usually drive more carefully?
   I've read that older people drive more carefully.

GIVING OPINIONS AND AGREEING

I've heard that a 16-year-old drives faster.
   So have I.
I think older people drive more slowly.
   So do I.

TALKING ABOUT QUALITY AND PERFORMANCE

Which machine washes better, the Quickwash or the SureSpeed?
   The Quickwash washes better.
Which washing machine runs the most economically?
   The SureSpeed runs the most economically of all.
Why is it the most economical?
   Because it takes only 18 minutes and it uses less water than the
   other machines.

TALKING ABOUT HYPOTHETICAL SITUATIONS

What would you do if you saw a robber in a bank?
   I'd call the police.
How would you feel if a friend lied to you?
   I'd be very upset.

GIVING REASONS

The ad says the Quickwash washes better.
I think we should buy a Quickwash because it uses less water.
If I had to buy a washing machine, I'd get the SureSpeed because it
runs more economically.

CONVINCING SOMEONE TO DO SOMETHING

Would you go to Los Angeles with me if I paid for everything?
   I guess so.

TALKING ABOUT FUTURE PLANS

What are you going to do during the school break?
   I hope to go camping.

IRREGULAR VERBS

Base Form	Simple Past	Past Participle
be	was, were	been
become	became	become
begin	began	begun
bite	bit	bitten
break	broke	broken
bring	brought	brought
build	built	built
buy	bought	bought
catch	caught	caught
choose	chose	chosen
come	came	come
cost	cost	cost
cut	cut	cut
do	did	done
draw	drew	drawn
drink	drank	drunk
drive	drove	driven
eat	ate	eaten
fall	fell	fallen
feed	fed	fed
feel	felt	felt
fight	fought	fought
fly	flew	flown
forget	forgot	forgotten
get	got	gotten
give	gave	given
go	went	gone
grow	grew	grown
have	had	had
hear	heard	heard
hit	hit	hit
hold	held	held
hurt	hurt	hurt
keep	kept	kept
know	knew	known

Base Form	Simple Past	Past Participle
leave	left	left
lend	lent	lent
lose	lost	lost
make	made	made
meet	met	met
pay	paid	paid
put	put	put
read	read	read
ride	rode	ridden
ring	rang	rung
run	ran	run
say	said	said
see	saw	seen
sell	sold	sold
send	sent	sent
shut	shut	shut
sing	sang	sung
sit	sat	sat
sleep	slept	slept
speak	spoke	spoken
spend	spent	spent
stand	stood	stood
steal	stole	stolen
swim	swam	swum
take	took	taken
teach	taught	taught
tell	told	told
think	thought	thought
throw	threw	thrown
understand	understood	understood
wake up	woke up	woke/woken up
wear	wore	worn
win	won	won
write	wrote	written

COMMON TWO-WORD VERBS

SEPARABLE TWO-WORD VERBS

ask out (ask someone for a date)
break down (stop working—for example, a car)
bring about (cause)
bring up (mention a subject; raise children)
call back (return a phone call)
call off (cancel)
call up (call on the phone)
check out (investigate; take a book out of
    the library)
cheer up (make someone feel better)
clean up (clean)
cross out (draw a line through)
cut out (stop doing something; remove something
    with a knife or scissors)
do over (repeat)
drop off (leave someone or something at a place)
figure out (solve a prolem; find an answer)
fill in/out (complete)
fill up (fill completely)
find out (discover)
get up (make someone leave his or her bed)
give back (return)
give up (surrender)
hand in (give something to a teacher or boss)
hand out (distribute)
hang up (put on a hook or hanger; return the
    telephone receiver)
have on (wear)
keep out (of) (not enter)
kick out (of) (make someone leave)
leave out (omit)
look over (examine)
look up (look for information in a book)
make out (see clearly)
make up (invent or create; do past work)
name after/for (give someone the name
    of someone else)
pass out (distribute; faint)
pay back (return money)
pick out (choose)
pick up (lift; clean; go and get someone)
point out (to) (show)
put away (return something to its place)
put back (return something to its place)
put off (postpone)
put on (put clothes on the body)
put out (extinguish a fire)
shut off (stop a machine)
stand up for (support)

start over (begin again)
take down (destroy, lower)
take off (remove clothes from the body)
take on (challenge; begin something new)
take out (take someone on a date; remove)
take over (gain control)
take up (begin discussing)
talk over (discuss)
tear down (destroy)
tear off (take a piece from something)
tear out (of) (remove a piece of page from a book)
tear up (tear into small pieces)
think over (consider)
throw away/out (throw into the garbage)
throw up (vomit)
try on (put on clothes to check the size, etc.)
try out (try; test)
turn down (decrease the volume)
turn in (give an assignment to the teacher;
    go to bed)
turn off (stop a machine or light)
turn on (start a machine or light)
turn out (extinguish a light)
turn up (increase the volume)
use up (finish)
wake up (make someone stop sleeping)
wear out (use or operate something until it isn't
    good or doesn't work)
write down (write something on a piece of paper)

INSEPARABLE TWO-WORD VERBS

break down (stop working)
call on (visit)
*catch up (with) (reach the same position)
check in/into (register at a hotel)
check into (investigate)
check out (of) (leave a hotel)
come across (meet by chance)
*come back (return)
*come over (come to one's house)
*come through (succeed)
*come to (regain consciousness)
cut down (on) (decrease the use of something)
*drop by (come and visit)
drop in (on) (stop and visit)
drop out (of) (stop attending)
fool around (with) (play but not seriously)
get along (with) (progress; interact)
*get back (return)

get in/into (enter a car, taxi, etc.; arrive)
get off (leave a bus, etc.)
get on (enter a plane, bus, etc.)
get out (of) (leave a place or a car)
get over (recover)
*get up (leave one's bed)
get through (with) (finish)
*give up (stop trying)
*go back (return)
*go on (begin; continue)
go over (review)
*grow up (become an adult)
*keep on (continue)
keep up (with) (stay at the same position)
*lie down (lie on a bed)
look after (take care of)
look for (search)
look into (investigate)
*look out (be careful)
*move back (return to where one used to live;
    make a room)
*pass away (die)
*pass out (lose consciousness, faint)
put up (with) (tolerate)
run across (discover by chance)
run into (meet by chance)
run out (of) (use the complete supply of something)
*sit down (stop standing and sit)
*show up (appear; come)
*stand up (stop sitting or lying and stand)
stay out (of) (not participate; not enter)
take after (resemble)
*take off (leave)
talk about (discuss)
*turn out (come, go)
wait on (serve)
*wake up (stop sleeping)
*warm up (get ready; exercise for a short time)
watch out (for) (be careful)
*work out (exercise)

*Intransitive verbs (they are not followed by an object).

TAPESCRIPTS
for Listening Comprehension Exercises

Lesson 1, exercise 7, p. 5

Victor is talking to a cashier in the school bookstore. First try to guess the missing words. Then listen and check your guesses.

Cashier: You aren't from here, are you?
Victor: No, I'm from Madrid.
Cashier: How long have you been in Dallas?
Victor: I've been here since Saturday. I've only been in the States for a couple of months.
Cashier: Really? You haven't been here for very long. How long have you studied English? Your English is very good.
Victor: I've studied English for about ten years—since I was thirteen.
Cashier: Well, I've studied Spanish since I was in eighth grade, and I still can't speak it!

Lesson 2, exercise 6, p. 9

Listen and complete the sentences with *could* or *couldn't*.

When I was a kid, I used to waste a lot of time. I never used to study or do my homework. I couldn't play any sports, and I didn't have any hobbies. I was lazy. I only used to play with my dog.

When I began high school, I realized it was important to study and to be successful in life. Today, I'm a nurse and I'm lucky. When I was younger, I couldn't solve a chemistry problem. Today, I can. I couldn't speak English either, but now I can. And I couldn't swim or play tennis. I could cook, but not very well. But today I can do all of those things. And I can do them very well. I can even use a computer!

Lesson 3, exercise 1, p. 10

Listen and choose the correct answer.

A: Who's that?
B: Oh, That's Hans Schmidt. He's from Germany, from Berlin. He's been in the United States for about four months. He arrived in Dallas on Sunday.
A: Does he speak English?
B: Yes. He speaks it very well. He's studied English since fifth grade.
A: Is he married?
B: Yes. His wife is in Germany. They've been married since 1989. And they have a son.
A: When was their son born?
B: In December . . . . Hans plays in a band in Germany. He's a very good musician. In fact, he's studied music since 1980, and he's played the saxophone for 10 years.
A: Does he have any other interests or hobbies?
B: No. He used to play soccer in high school, but he doesn't play now.

Lesson 1, exercise 5, p. 16

Listen and complete this conversation.

Lynn: Well, let's think. What do you enjoy doing?

Keiko: Well, I enjoy traveling.

Lynn: That's a good start. What about being a flight attendant?

Keiko: I can't do that part time. Besides, I'm afraid of flying.

Lynn: Do you like working outside? I know you love flowers.

Keiko: No. I'm not really interested in doing that. I can't stand working in the sun.

Lynn: Are you worried about making a lot of money?

Keiko: Not really. I'm just looking forward to getting a new job. I'm good at doing clerical work, but I'm tired of having the same routine every day.

Lesson 2, exercise 2, p. 18

Listen to Keiko's interview with Jessica Holloway. What things does Keiko like and dislike? What things didn't she mention?

Jessica: You must be Ms. Abe.

Keiko: That's right.

Jessica: And you're looking for a part-time job. Is that right?

Keiko: Yes.

Jessica: Tell me about yourself. What do you do now? And what are your interests?

Keiko: Well, I work in an office now, but I really don't like it. I'm bored with sitting at a desk all day.

Jessica: You mean you're tired of typing and filing and answering the phone all day.

Keiko: That's right. I can do those things, but I don't like having a daily routine. I like having responsibility, and I enjoy meeting new people.

Jessica: Then you are good at working with people?

Keiko: Yes. I like working with people.

Jessica: Why would you like to work in the fashion business?

Keiko: Well, I've always loved clothes. In fact, I enjoy sewing and making my own clothes. Also, I have a background in business and I'm good at working with numbers.

Jessica: Do you have any other interests?

Keiko: I enjoy traveling very much, and I'm interested in cooking.

Lesson 3, exercise 4, p. 22

First look at the pictures of the people below and read the information about them in the chart in exercise 5 on page 23. Then listen and find out which person got the job.

A: How about Albert Wu? He's got excellent qualifications.

B: But he doesn't like traveling, does he?

A: No, but he likes selling and he likes helping people, and he was a salesman before.

B: Georgia Hall worked in a school. That's good experience for this kind of work.

A: No. She doesn't like clerical work or working with numbers.

B: What do you think about hiring Greg Otero?

A: I think he could do the job. He enjoys working independently, and he likes having responsibility.

B: Yes, but he hates working for large companies, and he isn't interested in traveling.

A: That's not really true. He doesn't like flying, but he could take the train or drive to most places. And he used to work in a college bookstore. The job is perfect for him.

B: You're right, he sounds good. Is there anyone else?

A: Not really. There's Susan White. But she doesn't like selling at all. And we need a good salesperson.

B: OK. Why don't you call Greg and tell him he can have the job.

A: Good. I'm sure he'll be pleased.

Lesson 1, exercise 5, p. 29

Lynn is talking to Gina's fiance, Frank. Listen and choose the words you hear.

Lynn: You know, I love going to weddings—especially the receptions. I like to have a good time, and I love to dance.

Frank: Well, I hope you have a good time at our wedding. I prefer to have a big wedding, but Gina wants a small one.

Lynn: Oh, a small wedding will be nice. When are you going to start planning the reception.

Frank: Soon, I think. In fact, I think Gina is going to ask for your help. You know Gina—she hates organizing parties.

Lynn: Yeah, and she'll probably continue to work until the last minute, too, so she'll need some help.

Frank: You're right.

Lynn: Well, I'd be glad to help. In fact, I'm going to begin thinking about it right now.

Frank: That's great, because I can't stand to plan parties either.

Lesson 2, exercise 5, p. 32

It's the week before Gina's wedding. Gina is talking to Lynn and Keiko. Listen and check the things they have done. Then listen again and write when they did them.

Gina: I'm nervous. Do we have everything? Have you bought the champagne yet?

Lynn: No, we haven't. We're going to buy it tomorrow.

Gina: Have you ordered the food yet?

Lynn: Of course we have. We ordered it two weeks ago.

Gina: What about glasses? Have you bought the glasses yet?

Keiko: No. I'm going to get them when I buy the champagne.

Gina: Have you gotten the decorations yet?

Lynn: Yes. We've already gotten the decorations. We got them yesterday.

Gina: And the flowers?

Keiko: Yes. Oscar has promised to pick up the flowers. I ordered them last Tuesday.

Gina: Have you hired the band yet?

Lynn: Yes. We hired the band last week.

Gina: Have you ordered the cake?

Lynn: Yes, we have. We ordered it two weeks ago.

Gina: Let's see. Is there anything else? Oh, yes. Have you gotten the rice?

Keiko: Rice?

Gina: Yes. You know. It's traditional to throw rice at weddings in the States.

Keiko: Oh, well, no. We haven't gotten the rice yet.

Lesson 3, exercise 3, p. 34

What are they thinking? Listen and complete the sentences.

1. What am I doing here?
2. I enjoy being single!
3. I didn't plan to get married.
4. Stop worrying. Everything will be OK.
5. Look at him! He's a very handsome groom.

6. I have to stop shaking.
7. I can't stand being so nervous!
8. Look at her! She's really a beautiful bride.
9. Did I forget to bring her ring?
10. Relax! You know you'll enjoy living with her for the rest of your life.

Lesson 1, exercise 7, p. 41

Victor is talking to Lucy. Listen and complete the conversation.

Victor: My wife has decided to come and visit next month.

Lucy: Great!

Victor: Yeah, we'd like to stay here in Dallas for a few days and then we'd like to go to Los Angeles.

Lucy: Have you ever been to Los Angeles before?

Victor: No, I haven't.

Lucy: Has your wife ever been there?

Victor: No. She's never been there either.

Lesson 2, exercise 6, p. 45

Simon is talking to a friend. Listen and check where Simon has been.

Friend: So, have you decided about your vacation yet?

Simon: I guess we're going to Paris. We've never been there before.

Friend: Have you traveled a lot?

Simon: Yeah, I guess so. I've traveled in Mexico and Central America. And I've been to South America. But I've never gone to Europe or Asia . . . or Africa.

Friend: Where have you been in Central and South America?

Simon: Well, I've been to Guatemala. And I've been to Brazil.

Friend: I'd like to travel more. I've only been to Canada and Hawaii.

Simon: I like Canada. I was there a couple of years ago. It's a nice place for a vacation.

Friend: Have you ever been to Hawaii? My wife and I had a great time there last winter.

Simon: Yeah, I went there once. It's beautiful, but I don't really like beaches very much.

Lesson 3, exercise 3, p. 47

Listen and complete the conversation.

Customer A: We'd like to go someplace warm.

Travel Agent: Have you ever been to Bali?

Customer B: No, we haven't.

Travel Agent: Well, Bali may be a good place to go. It's a fascinating island with 20,000 temples and gorgeous beaches.

Customer B: But we don't know anything about the place.

Customer A: And we don't know anyone there.

Travel Agent: You shouldn't worry about that. There are a lot of tourists there. And the people are very friendly.

Customer A: Well, it sounds nice.

Travel Agent: It is. And if you decide to go, you really ought to visit the Denpasar Museum and market.

Lesson 1, exercise 6, page 53

One of the other teachers at the Language Institute isn't very polite. Listen and write down the teacher's orders.

1. All right. Pull the window shades down.
2. Now turn the VCR on.
3. Good. Now put the cassette in.
4. Wait a minute. Hey you! Turn your radio off.
5. And take your hat off.
6. And you! Put your glasses on.
7. OK. No wait! First pick these empty soda cans up.
8. Good. Now try the VCR out.
9. John! Take your pen out.
10. OK. Ready? Write everything I say down.

Lesson 2, exercise 4, p. 55

Tony and Roberto were watching a football game at 4:00 yesterday afternoon. What about their friends? Listen and match the two parts of the sentences.

1. Pravit was washing his car at 4:00 yesterday afternoon. (a)
2. Pravit's wife was working at the museum at that time. (e)
3. Olga was reading a magazine. (g)
4. Oscar was playing tennis. (b)
5. Lynn and Keiko were cooking dinner. (f)
6. Gina and Frank were watching TV. (h)
7. Lucy was working in the garden. (c)
8. Victor was studying. (d)

Lesson 3, exercise 2, page 57

At 4:00 someone turned the lights off in the museum. What were the people doing when the lights went out? Listen and answer True or False.

1. The woman with the big bag was standing by the drinking fountain when the lights went out.
2. The man with the mustache was leaning against the wall.
3. The young man with the brochure was standing near the restrooms.
4. The woman and the little boy were sitting on a bench.
5. The girl with the doll was lying on a bench.
6. The man in the wheelchair was looking at a statue.
7. The woman with the notebook was copying a painting.
8. The elderly man and woman were standing under the window.

Lesson 1, exercise 2, page 63

Listen and look at the example. Then listen and complete the other sentences with the correct form of the verb *be*.

Example: I wasn't able to fix the lawn mower, so I couldn't mow the lawn.

1. I was able to put up the window shades, but I couldn't put the curtains up.
2. They'll be able to meet us after the football game, so we'll tell them the news then.
3. She won't be able to help clean the basement because she won't be here when you're ready to begin.
4. He won't be able to play baseball with us this afternoon. He has to do some chores around the house.
5. If they aren't able to fix the car today, they can fix it tomorrow.
6. They weren't able to get here on time, so we began without them.

Lesson 2, exercise 5, page 70

Isabel is at Sandy's house. Listen and complete the conversation.

Sandy: Are you hungry?
Isabel: Yeah. I haven't had lunch yet. Could you make me a sandwich?
Sandy: Sure. I'll make it for you in a minute.
Isabel: And could you get me something to drink, too?
Sandy: Yeah. Could you show me your English homework while you're eating?
Isabel: Sure. Let me get it.
Sandy: Oh, could you lend me a pen? I can't find mine.
Isabel: Here. This sandwich is delicious.
Sandy: Thanks.
Isabel: Could you pass the salt and pepper? Thanks.

Lesson 3, exercise 3, page 72

Listen and then choose the correct words in parentheses.

Woman: How was the movie?
Man: I didn't like it. The story wasn't very interesting.
Woman: I'm sorry you were disappointed.
Man: Me, too. I didn't enjoy myself at all.
Woman: Who did you go with?
Man: I went by myself . . . . How was the museum?
Woman: We were fascinated. The paintings were very exciting.
Man: I'm glad you enjoyed yourselves.
Woman: We are, too.
Man: Who did you go with?
Woman: My husband and I went by ourselves. . . . And how was that new restaurant you went to?
Man: I was disappointed. The food wasn't exciting at all.
Woman: I'm sorry you didn't like it.
Man: Me, too. I didn't enjoy myself at all.
Woman: Who did you go with?
Man: I went with my girlfriend.

Lesson 1, exercise 3, page 78

Now listen and write what you hear. Listen to the example.

Example: (a cat meowing)

a. (a horse galloping)
b. (a telephone ringing)
c. (a piano playing simple melody)
d. (a train traveling on tracks, no whistle)
e. (ocean waves breaking on beach)
f. (someone typing)

Lesson 2, exercise 4, page 82

Listen and complete the conversations.

1. A: Lucy's cake was very sweet.
   B: But didn't you have a second piece? I thought you did.
   A: Yes, I did. I was being polite.

2. A: They didn't have enough sugar for the recipe.
   B: Did they buy some more?
   A: No, they didn't. They didn't make the cake.

3. A: Victor bought a new car.
   B: Oh, really? Is it nice?
   A: Yes, it looks very nice.

4. A: My class starts at 6:30.
   B: It's already 6:25. Won't you be late?
   A: Yes, but the teacher is always late.

5. A: Would you like to go see *Rain Man*?
   B: Haven't you seen it already? I thought you went last week.
   A: I did, but I want to see it again.

6. A: Don't you live in Dallas? I think I've seen you there.
   B: Yes, I do.
   A: I thought so.

Lesson 3, exercise 4, page 87

Two friends are talking on the phone. One is giving the other her recipe for carrot cake. Listen and complete the recipe.

Woman 1: Preheat the oven to three hundred and fifty degrees.
Woman 2: Three-fifty?
Woman 1: Uh-huh. Then grease two 9-inch round cake pans or one 9-inch by 13-inch pan.
Woman 2: OK.
Woman 1: Then with an electric mixer, beat the eggs, oil, and sugar. With the mixer on low, add the flour, baking soda, spices, and salt.
Woman 2: Sorry. Add the flour, baking soda, and what?
Woman 1: Add the flour, baking soda, spices, and salt.
Woman 2: Then what?
Woman 1: With a spoon, stir in the carrots, raisins, walnuts, and vanilla.
Woman 2: OK.
Woman 1: Then pour the mixture into the pans and bake for 35 minutes or until a toothpick comes out clean.
Woman 2: How long do you bake it?
Woman 1: For 35 minutes.
Woman 2: Anything else?
Woman 1: No. Just cool the cake for 10 minutes, and then remove it from the pans.
Woman 2: Great. I can't wait to try it.

Lesson 1, exercise 3, page 92

Listen and write the sentences.

1. Listen to this. Russia is larger than China.
2. Vatican City is smaller than the Philippines.
3. Mexico City is bigger than Tokyo.
4. The Pacific Ocean is bigger than the Atlantic.
5. The Nile River is longer than the Amazon.
6. Mt. Everest is higher than Mt. Fuji.
7. The Sahara Desert is larger than the Gobi Desert.
8. The Caspian Sea is bigger than Lake Superior.

Lesson 2, exercise 4, page 96

Listen for the correct information. Write numerals (10), not words (ten).

1. About 695,000,000 people speak Mandarin Chinese.
2. Approximately 400,000,000 people around the world speak English.
3. Ten percent or more of the people in 45 different countries speak English.
4. There were about 285,723,398 telephones in the world in 1984.
5. In 1984, there were also approximately 411,113,000 cars in the world.
6. The Japanese National Railways carries 18.8 million people every day.
7. The best-selling record album of all time is *Thriller* by Michael Jackson. It has sold more than 38.5 million copies.
8. Every day the world's population increases by 215,850, or 149.9, people per minute.

Lesson 3, exercise 1, page 97

First try to guess the missing words. Then listen and check your guesses.

THE UNITED STATES

The United States is a large country. It is 3,623,420 square miles. The United States lies between the Pacific and Atlantic oceans. The country to the north is Canada. The country to the south is Mexico. The capital of the United States is Washington, D.C. The United States is divided into 50 states, and each state has its own capital city.

The population of the United States is almost 250,000,000. The population includes people of almost every race, religion, and nationality. Although English is the common language, many people speak Chinese, Spanish, Italian, and other languages.

The geography of the United States is extremely varied. There are mountains, rivers, lakes, deserts, plains, and forests. The most important mountain ranges are the Appalachian Mountains in the east and the Rocky Mountains in the west. The most important rivers are the Mississippi River and the Missouri River in the middle of the country, and the Colorado and Columbia rivers in the west. The Rio Grande is the border between the United States and Mexico. The largest lakes are the Great Lakes between Canada and the United States.

Lesson 1, exercise 6, page 105

Gina and Frank are having lunch. Listen and complete their conversation.

Gina: Frank, we've got a problem. We don't have enough money to pay the rent this month.

Frank: I know. I guess I'd better ask Mom and Dad for a loan.

Gina: And I'd better ask my boss for a raise.

Frank: Do you think you'll get it?

Gina: I don't know. But maybe I'd better not take another English course for a while.

Frank: Gina, you can't stop studying English. It's important. This is an English-speaking country. You can't get ahead without English.

Gina: I know.

Frank: I'd better get a part-time job. I can work at the office during the day and then do something else at night. In fact, I'd better check the newspaper right now.

Lesson 2, exercise 2, page 107

Listen to each sentence. Write the city or country and the date.

1. The Statue of Liberty was given to the United States in 1885.
2. The Eiffel Tower was built in Paris in 1889.
3. The Golden Gate Bridge was built in San Francisco in 1937.
4. The Empire State Building was built in New York in 1931.
5. The Pyramids were built in Egypt around 2500 B.C.
6. The Sears Tower was built in Chicago in 1974.
7. The temples at Angkor Wat were built in Kampuchea in the twelfth century.
8. Corcovado was built in Rio de Janeiro in 1931.
9. The Sydney Opera House was built in Sydney in 1973.
10. The Colosseum was built in Rome in 80 A.D.

Lesson 3, exercise 1, page 109

Listen to the tour guide and write the dates you hear.

Good morning, ladies and gentlemen. Today's tour is called the President's Tour. Today we are going to visit the monuments and buildings that are dedicated to some of our most famous presidents.

First, we will stop at the Washington Monument. The Washington Monument was completed in 1884. It is dedicated to our first president, George Washington, and it is 555 feet high. You can take an elevator to the top or, of course, you can climb to the top—but there are 898 steps!

Next, we'll visit the White House, the official home of our present president. It was designed by James Hoban. The first building was burned by the British in the War of 1812, but it was rebuilt and painted white in 1818.

The Lincoln Memorial, our next stop, is dedicated to Abraham Lincoln, the sixteenth president of the United States. It was built in 1922. In the great hall there is a huge statue of Lincoln by Daniel Chester French.

Our last stop this morning will be at the . . . (fade out)

Lesson 1, exercise 5, page 117

Tony is reading a letter from his sister. First try to guess the missing words. Then listen and check your guesses.

Dear Tony,

Mom told me you are planning to go to the Grand Canyon with your friend Pierre. The Grand Canyon is an incredible place. It's really beautiful. I went there when I was in the U.S. However, if I were you, I'd go in the summer. I wouldn't go in the winter. The Grand Canyon is very cold in the winter, and I don't think you'd enjoy yourself if you went then. Also, if it snowed, you wouldn't be able to walk around and see things very well.

If I were you, I'd go someplace warm. In fact, I'd think about going to California. Maybe one of the other students would drive if you offered to pay for the gas. Maybe Pierre would go too if you asked him. I mean, if you told him you'd go to the Grand Canyon next summer, he'd probably go to California with you during your class break. Wouldn't you like all of that sunny weather and the beaches? I know I would!

Let me know what you decide.

Love,
Paula

Lesson 2, exercise 2, page 119

Are the sentences in the article from *Consumer Magazine* drawing conclusions *(must)*, giving advice *(should/ought to)*, talking about possibility *(might/may)*, or talking about ability (can). Complete the article with the appropriate words. Then listen and check your answers.

THE COMET IS BEST FOR DESIGN, ECONOMY, AND PERFORMANCE

Does your old car make a lot of noise? Does it use a lot of gas? Does it drive badly on the highway? Then you **must** need a new car.

Before you buy a new car, however, you really should take a look at the new Comet. You might be surprised by this year's model. It has a new engine, and it doesn't use much gasoline. It is the most efficient car on the market.

Besides the new engine, there are several new colors of paint and special matching interiors. You can choose evening gray, sunset red, midnight blue, or cloud white. You can select matching leather or plastic seats. And every car today ought to have a stereo cassette player, so every new Comet has one at no extra cost.

You should not buy a car if it doesn't drive smoothly, and you might not be happy if your new car uses too much gas. So we suggest that you drive the Comet and test it for yourself. You might like the way it handles. It steers easily and brakes well. And it is economical on gas.

If you don't choose a Comet, you must not be worried about economy and performance. And you must not need to think about price.

Lesson 3, exercise 4, page 122

Mr. Stein is talking to his class. What are his students going to do during class break? Listen and find out.

Mr. Stein: What are you going to do during the break, John?

John: I have a job. I'm going to play my guitar part time in a band.

Mr. Stein: How about you, Anna? What are you going to do?

Anna: I don't know yet. It depends on Laura. If she buys a new car, we'll probably drive to California.

Mr. Stein: And you, Maria?

Maria: I hope to go camping.

Mr. Stein: Oh, really? Camping should be fun. Where do you plan to go?

Maria: The Grand Canyon.

Mr. Stein: Oh, that's a beautiful place. But it might be cold. Would you go if it snowed?

Maria: Sure. That wouldn't matter.

Mr. Stein: How about you, Peter? Are you going anywhere?

Peter: My kids want to see their grandparents so I'm going back to New York to visit my parents.

Mr. Stein: Oh, that's nice. Is anyone else going home to visit his or her family?

Pablo: I am.

Mr. Stein: Well, have a good time, Pablo. You too, Peter.

Pablo: Thank you.

Mr. Stein: And you, Alex? Any plans?

Alex: I'm planning a trip to New Orleans.

Mr. Stein: New Orleans? That should be fun. How about you, Sue?

Sue: I have to work. My husband does, too. So we're staying here in Dallas. Besides, I don't feel like going anywhere right now.

Mr. Stein: Well, I hope you all enjoy yourselves and get some rest. And I'll look forward to seeing you again after the break.